A PHILOSOPHER READS...

Marvel Comics'

Thor

If They Be Worthy

Mark D. White

Published in 2022 by Ockham Publishing in the United Kingdom

ISBN: 978-1-83919-394-1

Cover by Claire Wood

www.ockham-publishing.com

To my dear friend Jane—yes, that's her real name—who beat cancer
and will always be my hero.

Acknowledgments

I would like to thank Rob Johnson at Ockham Publishing, who has been an endlessly supportive (and patient) editor and collaborator in the development of this book, Emily Vousden and Sarah Hembrow for their careful editing, and Claire Wood for the stunning cover. I would also like to thank a number of my friends, starting with Lauren Hale, Carol Borden, and Anita Leirfall, who as always provided endless support and encouragement; William Irwin, who gave me my start in writing on superheroes and philosophy and has been a sounding board ever since; Steve Nemeckay, who has kept me in comics and stitches for the last decade plus; and Amy Hannon, who never fails to remind me why I do this.

I also owe a massive debt of gratitude to the many creators behind the comic book stories of Thor. There are far too many to mention here—most of them appear to the references at the end of the book—but any list must include Stan Lee and Jack Kirby, who gave us the Marvel Comics version of Asgard in all its glory; Walter Simonson, who first got me hooked on the adventures of the Mighty Thor; and J. Michael Straczynski, who brought him down to Earth for me (figuratively and literally).

The most important creators for the purposes of this book are Jason Aaron, who wrote the seven years of Thor stories that are its primary focus, and his unparalleled group of artistic collaborators, especially Esad Ribić, Russell Dauterman, Olivier Coipel, Ive Svorcina, and Matthew Wilson (the MVP of comics colorists), who illustrated most of the stories discussed here. Together they chronicled the interwoven adventures of Thor Odinson and Jane Foster in fascinating philosophical and emotional complexity, combining words and images inextricably as can be done only in the medium of comics. Although I quote extensively from the dialogue and exposition in the original comics, unfortunately I cannot show the images that accompany them, and any feeble attempts I would make at describing them would not do them justice. I can only encourage you, after you read this book (and recommend it to all your friends, of course), to seek out the comics for yourself and revel in the stories as originally presented.

Contents

Introduction

Who among us has not doubted our worth or worthiness at some point in our lives? Maybe it was about our worth as a friend, family member, or romantic partner, and maybe it was as a student, employee, or volunteer. Maybe it was just an issue with our self-esteem or self-worth in general, leading us to feel inadequate in many areas of our lives. Whatever the context or degree, most of us, at one time or another, have felt we were not living up to a standard, whether set by others or by ourselves, and however reasonable (or not). When you don't feel worthy, it can be nearly impossible to do anything, to interact with other people, and to perform the most basic tasks, even picking up a pencil, a book, or...a hammer.

Consider Thor, the Asgardian God of Thunder and son of Odin the All-Father. (Yes, I know he's not the only Thor—I'm getting to that.) Thor must be judged worthy in order to lift his mighty hammer Mjolnir and command his full powers. Granted, his alternative is not too shabby: In the early comics, the Odinson would otherwise be Donald Blake, handsome and successful doctor, beloved by his nurse Jane Foster. In later years, other than brief periods in other mortal forms, he would remain his enormous Asgardian self, with his beloved hammer in his hand—and the worthiness it implied.

Being judged worthy by Mjolnir is, of course, very important to him, and it's not hard to see why, especially when we realize this goal was...ahem...hammered into him from a very early age. In general, everyone appreciates some occasional external validation, even when things seem to be going fairly well for them. Often, it's difficult to tell why people feel bad about themselves, especially when things look great for them from the outside. You may have just received a promotion at work, had your first child, or climbed your first mountain, and people would assume you're on top of the world (literally, if you just climbed a mountain). But none of that matters if *you* don't feel worthy, or if you see yourself as inferior, lacking in some way, or maybe even a loser. This is only compounded if you rely on someone else—or some*thing* else—to validate your worth for you, another entity with a mind of its own that makes judgments based on standards that may be irrelevant, unreasonable, or impossible.

Now imagine being Thor. After untold centuries of defending Asgard and the other realms from Frost Giants, Dark Elves, and the occasional Fire Demon, you suddenly find yourself judged unworthy by your beloved hammer. You're unable to lift it, or even budge it, and then you discover someone else was able to lift it and has taken your place as the new Thor. (Never mind that Thor is actually his name—we'll get to that too.) On occasion, other people have been able to lift the hammer momentarily, most notably Captain America, but even he didn't "become the new Thor" when he did it. (As you may know, Cap prefers a shield anyway.) One notable exception is Beta Ray Bill, an alien from the planet Korbin who fought Thor and picked up Mjolnir, transforming into a larger, armored version of himself. Normally, whenever someone other than Thor manages to lift the hammer, it's merely an affirmation of their worthiness. But this time, when the Odinson was found unworthy, a new Thor appeared after she lifted the hammer, sending the original into an emotional and philosophical tailspin—one we will explore in this book.

What about this new Thor? Don't think we've forgotten about her— she's a big part of this book as well. After months of secrecy and false leads, she was revealed to be none other than Jane Foster, originally

Blake's nurse and love interest, who had since become a doctor herself and remained in Thor's life as a valued colleague and confidante. While the Odinson was struggling with unworthiness, Jane was undergoing chemotherapy to fight cancer, only to have her progress stalled each time she transformed into the Mighty Thor.

Why did Mjolnir regard Jane as worthy and the Odinson as unworthy? Had something about the Odinson changed, or did Mjolnir "change its mind" about what it regarded as worthy? Does the Odinson become worthy again—and, if so, how? More generally, who (or what) is Mjolnir to be judging worthiness anyway? Who is the appropriate judge of worthiness, others or oneself? And most important, what does it mean to be worthy—and how might it be related to unworthiness?

All these questions and more are raised in the seven years of Marvel Comics about Thor written by Jason Aaron and illustrated by a cadre of magnificent artists such as Russell Dauterman and Esad Ribić. In this book, we will follow the saga of these two Thors, as told by Aaron and his artistic collaborators, thinking about the philosophical concept of worthiness as we go.

We will start with how worthiness was understood in the early comics, which matches many of our basic intuitions about what makes a person worthy, but also leaves many questions that will be answered as we go on. When Aaron's run begins, we will see Thor begin to have doubts about his own worthiness as well as the worthiness of gods in general. This will raise the topic of what being a "god" means to an Asgardian and how this version of godhood can translate to our world. After the Odinson is declared unworthy, we will follow Jane Foster's tenure as Thor, exploring how and why Mjolnir regards her as worthy, as well as the ways her worthiness may be different from that of her predecessor. As she fights to assert herself as the new Thor on Earth as well as on Asgard—Odin is not a fan, to put it mildly—the original Thor is left to deal with his own unworthiness, which gives us the chance to discuss how one experiences and deals with such feelings and begins to combat them. Finally, we will come to a deeper understanding of worthiness alongside the Odinson, and watch as he rejoins Jane to fight beside her before she...well, let's leave something for later, shall we?

I'm excited that you've chosen to join me on this philosophical journey through one of the most fascinating and exciting storylines in a half-century of Thor comics. (And that includes the ones about the frog.) Jason Aaron and his artistic partners have given us a unique way to explore many dimensions of worthiness by observing how Thor Odinson and Jane Foster each deal with the burdens of being the God of Thunder, as well as why they were chosen—or, in the Odinson's case, rejected—as being worthy of the honor. I wrote this book to be enjoyed by anyone, whether you're new to Thor or philosophy, or you're a longtime fan of either (or both). Regardless, when you reach the end of the book, I hope that, not only will you feel entertained and have a deeper appreciation for the stories of Thor, but you will have new ways to think about any issues you may have about your own worth, value, or self-esteem.

Chapter 1: Thor and Worthiness

Although his backstory has grown and developed throughout his history, the basic concept of Thor in the Marvel Universe has remained roughly the same since his introduction in *Journey into Mystery* #83 in August 1962, especially after his canonical origin was told in 1983's *Thor Annual* #11. Based loosely on Norse mythology, Thor is from Asgard, one of the Ten Realms on Yggdrasil, the World Tree; another one of the realms is Midgard, which we know as Earth.[1] He is the son of Odin, the All-Father of Asgard and one of the mightiest beings in the universe, and Gaea, the Mother Goddess of Earth, although Odin's wife Freyja is the mother who loved and raised him.[2] Thor was raised as the presumptive heir to his father's throne, much to the consternation of his adopted brother, Loki, whom Odin raised as his own after killing Loki's father Laufey, King of the Frost Giants, in battle.[3] As he matured, Thor grew close to Sif, sister of Heimdall, the guardian of the rainbow bridge Bifrost; some of Loki's earliest mischief against Thor was taken out on Sif, such as when he cut off her long blonde hair and replaced it with black, only to be frustrated when Thor thought that even lovelier.[4]

From an early age, Thor reveled in glorious adventures throughout all the realms, often at the side of the Warriors Three: Fandral the Dashing, Hogun the Grim, and Volstagg the…well…Volstagginous. As much fun as he was having, however, Thor's ultimate goal was always to wield the mighty hammer Mjolnir, forged by the dwarves of Nidavellir from mystical Uru metal, and enchanted by Odin so it could be lifted only by one who was "worthy."[5] Thor's struggle to become worthy, to remain worthy, and to reclaim his worthiness after losing it, will be a central theme of this book as we go forward.

After Thor achieved worthiness and claimed Mjolnir as his own, Odin came to regard his son as arrogant, brash, and reckless, so he banished him to Earth in a human form he constructed named Donald Blake, a young doctor with an injured leg that required him to use a cane, with no knowledge of his earlier life in Asgard.[6] When Blake lost his cane while exploring the coast of Norway, he found a "gnarled wooden stick—like an ancient cane" in a cave, and after he struck it against a rock, he transformed into Thor (and the cane into Mjolnir).[7] Thor soon discovered that if he became separated from Mjolnir for longer than sixty seconds, he would revert to Blake—which was his main weakness, and one that would apply to future wielders of Mjolnir as well.

This "punishment" was designed to teach the young Thor humility and the importance of service to others—which it did, but it had another consequence that the All-Father would come to regret. Thor had always spent a lot of time on Midgard, enjoying the worship and company of Vikings in the "olden days," but living among mortals as one of them only strengthened Thor's bonds to Earth. Odin had long been uncomfortable with this, arguing with his son that he should spend more time on Asgard at his father's side, learning to rule as presumptive heir to the throne, and their arguments over this only became more fierce and frequent after Odin made Thor live on Earth fulltime.

Although he felt a close tie to Earth based on his maternal heritage, his long history with its people, and his relatively new friendship with the Avengers, Thor's deeper attachment to Earth had another explanation: Donald Blake's nurse, Jane Foster, who fell in love with both Blake and Thor before learning they were one and the same. Their relationship is one of the ongoing threads woven throughout the Thor comics, and was a thorn in Odin's side since the day he became aware of it, both because he did not regard Jane as a worthy mate for his son, and because their love only pulled his son away from Asgard more. When Thor told his father of his intention to marry Jane, Odin at first refused, later to relent on the condition that Jane become a god. After Jane agreed but could not adjust to godhood, Odin returned her to Earth with her memories of Asgard erased, and then re-introduced his son to his boyhood love Sif, who would be Thor's primary love interest for years to come (and kept him more tightly rooted to Asgard).[8] As we shall see in the next chapter, Jane would eventually get her comeuppance, achieving both godhood and the title of Thor—with the hammer to show for it.

What Does It Mean to Be "Worthy"?

Forged by dwarves from mystic Uru metal, in fires that would melt the sun. Laden with enchantments by the All-Father himself. Able to shatter whole planets as easy as pebbles. It is the most powerful weapon in all the nine realms. But only the worthy may lift it. I have wrestled dragons with my bare hands. Slain wolves the size of longboats. I have fought in more battles than most gods twice my age. So tell me...how much more worthy must I be?[9]

The lament above represents the young Thor's frustration at failing to satisfy the hammer's judgment despite performing labors that would astonish Hercules. Perhaps the problem lay not with him, though, but with the fact that he apparently didn't know exactly what it took to be worthy—and neither did we, the readers.

In the very first Thor story, the inscription on Mjolnir read: "Whosoever holds this hammer, if he be worthy, shall possess the power

7

of…Thor." Besides the pronoun, which changed to "she" when Jane Foster picked up the hammer (and later to the more inclusive "they"), this inscription has not changed since 1962. However, the precise meaning of what it means to be "worthy" has never been explained—in the same story, Thor suggests the hammer is simply too heavy for anyone else to lift, to say nothing of being worthy.[10] In fact, he refers only to the literal implication of the inscription, which demands that a worthy person hold the hammer to maintain the power of Thor, not that it takes a worthy person to lift it at all.[11]

About a year later, the issue of worthiness was mentioned for the first time when Thor was trying to figure out why his evil duplicate couldn't get the full power from the hammer (although he was able to lift it). He looks at the inscription and thinks to himself:

> That inscription on the hammer…"whosoever holds this hammer, if he be worthy, shall possess the power of Thor!"…That's the answer! "If he be worthy"!! That's why my duplicate, even if he held a hundred hammers, wouldn't be able to defeat me with them! He is an evil copy of me, therefore unworthy to possess my hammer's power![12]

Here, worthiness is contrasted with the duplicate's evil nature, implying that to be worthy means to be good in an ethical sense.

Is this our answer, then: To be worthy is to be ethical? Not quite, although it's a start. Moral philosophy is often said to boil down to the question of "what is good" or "how to be good," so this simply points us in the right direction.

Different schools of moral philosophy have their own unique ways to think about these questions. For instance, *consequentialism* looks at the outcomes (or consequences) of one's actions: To be good in a consequentialist way means doing things that have positive outcomes (the *most* positive outcomes) or avoiding doing things that have negative outcomes (or at least do the least harm you can). The most well-known version of consequentialism is *utilitarianism*, which assumes that good and bad outcomes are measurable and comparable, so ideally you can figure out the best action in any given situation by comparing the positive and negative effects of various options.[13] Iron Man, one of Thor's fellow Avengers, often makes decisions like a utilitarian: He computes the costs and benefits of dozens of possible solutions to any problem, based on his claim to be a "futurist" who can predict the outcomes of every option.[14]

Another approach to moral philosophy, which contrasts with consequentialism, is *deontology*, which focuses on doing the right thing rather than the best (or least bad) thing. To a deontologist, the right thing is determined by applying a moral principle to a general action, rather than considering the positive or negative outcomes of performing the action in a particular situation. For example, a consequentialist may say that lying is bad because it usually results in people getting hurt, whereas a deontologist would more likely say that lying is wrong because it fails to respect the person being lied to, using them as a means to an end rather than treating them as a valuable end in themselves.[15] Both lines of reasoning can result in a rule like "do not lie," but deontologists get there by thinking about the action itself and whether it corresponds to important principles such as respect and dignity, rather than whether its consequences will generally help or hurt people. Captain America can be described as a deontologist, thinking in terms of right and wrong rather than good and bad, and is often seen arguing with Iron Man about whether "the ends justify the means" when he wants to do something Cap thinks is wrong.[16]

Both consequentialism and deontology give us useful perspectives for deciding whether an action is ethical or not, but neither really gets to the heart of what makes a *person* good (or worthy). Are we good people because we do good things—or do we do good things because we're good people? A third school of moral philosophy, *virtue ethics*, takes the latter approach, focusing on a person's character and how it leads to ethical decisions and behavior. Specifically, virtue ethicists identify positive character traits or *virtues*, such as honesty, courage, and generosity, which help guide decision-making and action in a way that promotes "the good life" in terms of your own well-being as well as your contributions to society. To continue with our example of lying, honest people refrain from lying, not because it violates a rule, but because it goes against their moral character; they generally do the good or right thing in expression of a virtuous trait that they cultivated.[17]

Although this book is not about Thor's ethical code, it is safe to say that the Odinson's behavior is best described with virtue ethics.[18] It is difficult to imagine Thor calculating the optimal response to a problem, or weighing various principles, rights, and duties to solve a moral dilemma. Instead, we usually see him reacting to a situation—sometimes hastily, and not always wisely—based on character traits that have been honed through centuries of battle to reflect the expectations of Asgardian royalty: virtues such as courage, honesty, loyalty, and sacrifice.

At the same time, Thor clearly exhibits many traits that are not virtuous, such as arrogance, gluttony, and impatience. These "bad" character traits, or *vices*, can be thought of as excesses or insufficiencies of virtue: Arrogance is too much self-confidence, gluttony is too little temperance, impatience is (obviously) too little patience. True virtue, according to Aristotle, is the "golden mean" between two extremes. For example, the virtue of courage is found between the extremes of cowardice (too little) and foolhardiness (too much). Furthermore, the optimal degree of courage for each person is different: Thor can be reasonably expected to exhibit more courage than Donald Blake is, given their respective physical strength and abilities.

Despite their differences, all three ethical theories lead to many of the same judgments—lying, cheating, and killing are bad, for example, and helping others is good—although for different reasons and permitting of different exceptions. However, virtue ethics is the only one of the three that focuses on what makes a *person* good, as opposed to what makes certain actions good. It makes sense, then, that when we ask what makes someone worthy—say, to lift a certain hammer—virtue ethics would provide an intuitively satisfying answer.

What Do the Early Stories Say about Worthiness?

Most of the Thor comics treat worthiness as something obvious, along of the lines of "you know what it is when you see it" or "if you have to ask, you'll never understand." With all due respect to Justice Potter Stewart—who famously used the first phrase to describe obscenity in a 1964 United States Supreme Court case—philosophers are rarely satisfied with this sort of hand-waving, insisting on getting to the core of what a word or term means.[19] (We even have a name for it: *conceptual analysis*.)

It would be great if we could ask Odin, who placed the enchantment on the hammer to begin with, but unfortunately he has never cared to elaborate on what exactly he meant by "if he be worthy." Originally, Mjolnir was portrayed as mimicking the All-Father's judgment, granting itself, and the power of Thor, to whomever Odin would find worthy.[20] More recently, though, it has been strongly suggested that Mjolnir judges worthiness itself (as we'll see in the chapter 3), going so far as to deny Odin himself the ability to lift it. (And for all of his insistence that

11

his son learn humility, Odin has never been a big fan of the idea, so you can imagine how he took this.)

Appropriately, the earliest clue to what worthiness might mean comes in the story of how Thor first lifted Mjolnir, which appears in the "Tales of Asgard" back-up stories in *Journey into Mystery*, vol. 1, #100–102 (January–March 1964). The narration at the beginning of the first installment tells us that "accomplishing deeds of valor" is necessary for "inheriting the enchanted battle hammer of Odin." By the end, young Thor has done just that, defeating two Storm Giants to retrieve the Golden Apples of Idunn, which give Asgardians their strength and immortality. After his return to the palace, Thor finds that he can lift Mjolnir a tiny bit, and Odin assures him, "After each deed of valor, my son Thor, you are able to lift my hammer a little higher!"[21] This sentiment is echoed in the next story by young Thor himself, who insists on helping Heimdall protect the Bifrost; when his aid is rejected, he pleads, "But I must do noble deeds, that I may earn the mighty Uru hammer of Odin!"[22] And true to his father's word, after he helps to repel an invasion (instigated by Loki), Thor is able to lift the hammer a little higher.

Although both of these stories refer to deeds or accomplishments that Thor must perform to be deemed worthy, these actions are described in terms that reflect on the person doing them: valor and nobility. The latter may refer to Thor's royal lineage and the resulting expectations of him, which are ethically ambiguous but generously interpreted as virtuous (at least in cases of benevolent rulers). More familiar to us "commoners" is valor, a variant of courage, one of the classic virtues identified by Aristotle, although valor is often understood to refer to particularly heroic displays of courage, especially in battle.[23] After he finally lifts Mjolnir—more on that soon—Thor reflects on his accomplishment, remembering that his father told him, "When thou art finally ready, thou shalt not even feel the hammer's weight," and thinking to himself, "Truly did Odin speak that day…for when my courage rose to face the greatest challenge of all, I swung the enchanted hammer as lightly as if it were my boyish sword!"[24]

Courage is obviously an important trait for any hero to possess, but the Thor stories describe worthiness in terms of other virtues as well, even if rather vaguely. Once, during an adventure in Doctor Doom's kingdom of Latveria, Thor throws Mjolnir away to divert an incoming missile, and sixty seconds later he reverts to Donald Blake. When the hammer lands, Doom finds, much to his frustration, that he cannot lift it, so the petulant dictator puts a forcefield around it so no one else can try. When Donald finds the hammer, he digs under the forcefield to retrieve Mjolnir and become Thor once again. Watching from Asgard, Odin celebrates Thor's ingenuity, proclaiming, "Mjolnir hath been regained! My son hath proved his worth!"[25] Cleverness can definitely be considered a virtue, but it would more likely be classified as an *executive virtue*, one that helps us decide how to act on our core virtues. It could also be wrapped into the concept of practical wisdom (what Aristotle termed *phronêsis*) or *judgment*, which is necessary for all persons to translate their general virtues into definite action in specific circumstances. A relatable thread in the stories of the young Thor is the development of his faculty of judgment as he develops from young prince into mature hero, which should be familiar to everyone (especially parents!).[26]

One notable mention of worthiness arose in the context of someone else lifting Mjolnir—a colleague and friend about whom, earlier in the same issue, Thor says, "I have never known a mortal as honorable and noble."[27] During a case with the Avengers, the monstrous Grog separated Thor from his hammer—and was none too happy he failed to lift it himself—so it was up to Captain America, then operating as simply

"The Captain" after a disagreement with the U.S. government, to retrieve it for him. Despite his doubts, Cap is able to lift Mjolnir, use it to fight off more than a dozen attackers, and then toss it to its rightful owner. After the Avengers defeat Grog and his allies, Thor says to Cap, about wielding the mighty hammer, that "only a man or god worthy—pure of heart and noble of mind—could have done so!"[28] Unlike the previous emphasis on deeds and accomplishments, here the focus is on the person wielding the hammer, "pure of heart" and "noble of mind" both referring to fine moral character in general rather than specific virtues.[29]

How Did Thor Finally Lift Mjolnir?

Given that the early stories said one must perform "deeds of valor and nobility" to lift Mjolnir—which young Thor clearly has, countless times over—what is it that finally makes him worthy? Unfortunately for him, it wasn't simply a matter of doing *enough*: In one story before he won the hammer, he bemoans the fact that he just fought for nine days straight to save Earth, and is disappointed that even this isn't enough.[30]

In the third installment of the original story, the Fates—three sisters who, in both Norse and Greek mythology, plot the destinies of all living beings—tell young Thor that, before he can lift Mjolnir, "you have to meet death first!" When he returns to the royal palace, he learns from a bloodied Balder that the Storm Giants abducted Sif, and Thor swears, "I shall rescue Sif from the enemy, or die trying!" Following his oath, as the narration says, "Then, for the first time in his life, Thor grasps the mighty hammer and holds it high over his head!! But, so intent upon his mission is he that he doesn't realize what he is doing!" When he learns that the Storm Giants handed Sif over to Hela, the Goddess of Death and ruler of Hel, Thor immediately offers his life to her in exchange for Sif's, which Hela refuses, telling Thor "I cannot take a life which is so young, so brave, so noble!" The narration in the final panel reads: "And so it was that Thor first gained possession of his magic hammer—by offering to make the supreme sacrifice—giving up his life for that of another!"[31] When this story is retold later, we see a subsequent ceremony during which Odin proclaims: "For these and other deeds of selfless valor countless as the heaven's stars...enchanted Mjolnir is yours to wield with care, bold Thor, Asgard's heir apparent and my devoted son!"[32]

In this tale, we find three elements of basic worthiness as far as Mjolnir is concerned: selflessness, sacrifice, and "doing without thinking," which is to say, acting without self-awareness. The first two are obvious aspects of heroism, putting the life and safety of others above one's own, but the third is more specific to this case. We see it again in a later story of the young Thor's "first time" lifting Mjolnir: After he is brought to the present day to help the Asgardians in the War of the Realms (on which more later), he fights valiantly yet still cannot lift the older Thor's Mjolnir when he tries. But after he hears his mother Freyja scream, he absentmindedly grabs the hammer and takes off with it to save her, only realizing later what he has done.[33] Not only does it take a selfless act of sacrifice to make Thor worthy of lifting the hammer, but he also needs to do it without thinking—in particular, without consciously trying to be worthy enough to do it.

This idea of "mindless action" is reminiscent of *wei wu wei*, a concept from the ancient Chinese philosophy of *Taoism*. In his seminal book *Tao Te Ching*, philosopher Lao-Tzu cautioned against counterproductive effort, instead recommending that we "do nondoing, strive for nonstriving."[34] Although this sounds paradoxical to Western ears, it has many applications to modern life. For instance, the quest for happiness is often described in terms that resemble *wei wu wei*, such as the commonplace saying that you can't force happiness, but rather you need to do things that *make* you happy—in other words, achieving happiness without

15

thinking about it. The point is not to literally do nothing, but to avoid putting so much effort into something that it defeats the purpose, such as making yourself miserable trying to be happy. The quest for love is often discussed the same way: Rather than force it, we should make ourselves open to it by "putting ourselves out there" and letting things happen naturally.[35]

We can think of even more common examples. Most of us do simple things like getting dressed and tying our shoes without thinking, and when we do get distracted and have to think about what we're doing, we're often lost about what to do next. (Anyone who's tried to teach a young child how to tie their shoes knows how strange it is to actually think about how you do it.) More relevant to the case of Thor and his mighty hammer, people who have to react immediately to urgent situations, such as soldiers in battle or athletes in competition, are often described as doing so automatically, without conscious thought or deliberation, relying on extensive training and experience instead.[36]

What does this have to do with worthiness, though? After all, as we said, selflessness and sacrifice are obvious heroic virtues, but what is particularly virtuous about "doing without thinking"? The comics provide no answer, but one possible explanation is that action performed this way is not based on conscious deliberation, but rather an instinctive reaction based on a person's core character traits, and if the resulting action is selfless, courageous, or "noble," it serves as evidence that those traits have been successfully cultivated. The fact that Thor doesn't have to think about risking his life to save Sif or Freyja shows that doing so is a reflection of who he has become—and he is worthy for it.[37]

****

Because this is only the first chapter, you should expect that we have a lot more to say on the topic of worthiness. It definitely begins with unthinking selflessness and sacrifice, but it gets more complicated when Thor suddenly loses his worthiness and the ability to wield Mjolnir. This makes him (and us) wonder: What changed? Even after we learn *why* he became unworthy, there remains the task of *how* he becomes worthy again…and this time, it's going to take more than offering his life to save another.

[1] Traditionally there were nine realms, but recently it was revealed that Odin had expelled a tenth realm, Heven, from Yggdrasil and covered up its existence (*Original Sin* #5.1, September 2014).

[2] There has recently been speculation that the cosmic being known as the Phoenix is actually Thor's mother (in *Avengers*, vol. 8, #43, May 2021), but as of the time of writing this has yet to be confirmed.

[3] *Journey into Mystery*, vol. 1, #112 (January 1965), "Tales of Asgard: The Coming of Loki!" Thor has a number of other siblings, some he only recently became aware of, such as his old friend Balder the Brave, revealed to be his brother in *Thor*, vol. 3, #10 (September 2008), and Angela, raised as an angel of Heven and revealed to be his sister in *Original Sin* #5.1.

[4] *Thor Annual* (vol. 1) #11 (1983).

[5] Ibid.; as we shall see later, the origin of Mjolnir was retold and expanded in *The Mighty Thor*, vol. 2, #12 (December 2016).

[6] This was first explained in *Thor*, vol. 1, #159 (December 1968). Donald Blake eventually became a less important entity in the comics, disappearing for the most part after *Thor*, vol. 1, #340 (February 1984), only to reappear sporadically thereafter, perhaps most significantly when he and Thor had to seek out the other Asgardians in mortal form on Earth after Ragnarok, the mythological destruction of Asgard (*Thor*, vol. 3, #1, September 2007).

[7] *Journey into Mystery*, vol. 1, #83 (August 1962), "Thor the Mighty and the Stone Men from Saturn!"

[8] *Thor*, vol. 1, #136 (January 1967), "To Become an Immortal!"

[9] *Thor: God of Thunder* #2 (January 2013).

[10] *Journey into Mystery*, vol. 1, #83, "Thor the Mighty and the Stone Men from Saturn!"

[11] To be sure, Odin's intention was clear, albeit vague in its presentation: "Henceforth, no one shall be able to wield this hammer lest he be worthy…" (*Thor Annual*, vol. 1, #11). Later, the enchantment would be described as making it "all but impossible for anyone else to ever lift it" (*The Mighty Thor*, vol. 2, #12, December 2016), and Odin tells the young Thor the same: "Mjolnir is not to be touched. Not by anyone. It's far too powerful. And too Bor-damned wild!" (*Generations: The Unworthy Thor & The Mighty Thor* #1, October 2017). (Bor is Odin's father, so read into this what you will.)

[12] *Journey into Mystery*, vol. 1, #95 (August 1963), "The Demon Duplicators."

[13] For a thorough introduction to consequentialism, see Walter Sinnott-Armstrong's entry on the topic at the *Stanford Encyclopedia of Philosophy* (Summer 2019 Edition), Edward N. Zalta (ed.), at https://plato.stanford.edu/archives/sum2019/entries/consequentialism/. For the original work in utilitarianism specifically, see Jeremy Bentham, *The Principles of Morals and Legislation* (1781), available at https://www.utilitarianism.com/jeremy-bentham/, and John Stuart Mill's *Utilitarianism* (1863), available at https://www.utilitarianism.com/mill1.htm.

[14] For more on Iron Man's utilitarianism and its numerous complications, see Part I of my book *A Philosopher Reads Marvel Comics' Civil War: Exploring the Moral Judgment of Captain America, Iron Man, and Spider-Man* (Ockham Publishing, 2016).

[15] This language comes from Immanuel Kant, the most well-known deontologist, and one of the versions of his famous (or infamous) *categorical imperative*, his test to determine if plans of action conform to the moral law. The core of his ethical theory is put forward in his short book, *Grounding for the Metaphysics of Morals* (trans. James W. Ellington, Indianapolis, IN: Hackett Publishing Company, 1785/1993); for a useful introduction, see Roger J. Sullivan, *An Introduction to Kant's Ethics* (Cambridge: Cambridge University Press, 1994). On deontology in general, see Larry Alexander and Michael Moore's entry in the *Stanford Encyclopedia of Philosophy*, Winter 2020 Edition, Edward N. Zalta (ed.), at https://plato.stanford.edu/archives/win2020/entries/ethics-deontological/.

[16] And this happens *a lot*, as I discuss throughout the first two parts of *A Philosopher Reads Marvel Comics' Civil War* (covering Iron Man and Captain America, respectively).

[17] The most well-known proponent of virtue ethics is Aristotle, whose *Nicomachean Ethics* is available at http://classics.mit.edu/Aristotle/nicomachaen.html. On virtue ethics in general, see Rosalind Hursthouse and Glen Pettigrove, "Virtue Ethics," in *Stanford Encyclopedia of Philosophy* (Winter 2018 Edition), Edward N. Zalta (ed.), at https://plato.stanford.edu/archives/win2018/entries/ethics-virtue/.

[18] For a brief discussion of the different ethical codes of Iron Man, Captain America, and Thor, see my chapter "Superhuman Ethics Class with the Avengers Prime" in my edited volume *The Avengers and Philosophy: Earth's Mightiest Thinkers* (Hoboken, NJ: John Wiley & Sons, 2012), pp. 5–17. To be precise, Captain America is more complicated, displaying aspects of both deontology and virtue ethics in his behavior, as I explain in my book *The Virtues of Captain America: Modern-Day Lessons on Character from a World War II Superhero* (Hoboken, NJ: John Wiley & Sons, 2014).

[19] The case was *Jacobellis v. Ohio*, 378 U.S. 184 (1964); for more on Justice Stewart's famous phrase, see Peter Lattman, "The Origins of Justice Stewart's 'I Know It When I See It,'" in *The Wall Street Journal*, September 27, 2007, available at https://www.wsj.com/articles/BL-LB-4558.

[20] *Thor*, vol. 1, #400 (February 1989), "I...This Hammer! (Or, If You Knew Uru Like We Know Uru!)"

[21] *Journey into Mystery*, vol. 1, #100 (January 1964), "Tales of Asgard: The Storm Giants."

[22] *Journey into Mystery*, vol. 1, #101 (February 1964), "Tales of Asgard: The Invasion of Asgard."

[23] See section 4.1 of Aristotle's *Nicomachean Ethics* for his lengthy and impassioned discussion of courage.

[24] *Thor*, vol. 1, #252 (October 1976), "Tales of Asgard: The Weapon and the Warrior."

[25] *Thor*, vol. 1, #183 (December 1970). To be fair, this probably reflects lack of foresight on the part of Doctor Doom more than brilliance on the part of Thor!

[26] For more on superheroes and judgment, see chapter 5 in *The Virtues of Captain America* and my chapter "Moral Judgment: The Power That Makes Superman Human," in my edited book *Superman and Philosophy: What Would the Man of Steel Do?* (Hoboken, NJ: Wiley-Blackwell, 2013), pp. 5-15.

[27] *Thor*, vol. 1, #390 (April 1988).

[28] Ibid. And he did "do so" on several more occasions, including *Fear Itself #7*, "Thor's Day" (December 2011) and *Avengers*, vol. 8, #28 (February 2020), plus a small indie film you may have seen, called *Avengers: Endgame* (2019).

[29] After Thor proclaims a "sacred bond" between him and Cap based on wielding Mjolnir, Cap tells him "I hope I'll always be worthy of that honor and privilege, my friend!" (*Thor*, vol. 1, #390). Although Cap may not have meant "worthy" in the sense we're discussing it here, this does foreshadow developments later in this book regarding the importance of always striving to be worthy.

[30] *Generations: The Unworthy Thor & The Mighty Thor #1*.

[31] *Journey into Mystery*, vol. 1, #102 (March 1964), "Tales of Asgard: Death Comes to Thor."

[32] *Thor Annual*, vol. 1, #11.

[33] *Thor*, vol. 5, #14 (August 2019).

[34] Lao-Tzu, *Tao Te Ching*, Chapter 63, in Thomas Cleary (ed. and trans.), *The Taoist Classics Volume One* (Boston: Shambala, 1990), p. 38.

[35] For more examples of the relevance of *wei wu wei* today, and how it relates to both modern psychology and neuroscience, see Edward Slingerland's book *Trying Not to Try: Ancient China, Modern Science, and the Power of Spontaneity* (New York: Crown, 2015).

[36] There is some dispute regarding this: See Barbara Gail Montero's article "The Myth of 'Just Do It'" in *The New York Times*, June 9, 2013, at https://opinionator.blogs.nytimes.com/2013/06/09/the-myth-of-just-do-it/, based on her book *Thought in Action: Expertise and the Conscious Mind* (Oxford: Oxford University Press, 2016).

[37] Think of the movie *Captain America: The First Avenger* (2011), when scrawny Private Steve Rogers instinctively jumps on the grenade during basic training, not knowing it was a dud. He didn't think about it—it was just "in him" to do it, and that showed that he was worthy of receiving the Super-Soldier Serum and Vita-Rays that transformed him into Captain America.

Chapter 2: Thor and Godhood

> Small-g gods? Big-G? I don't know. Are the As-
> gardians "gods"? A whole lot of people sure
> seemed to think so not terribly long ago. And if
> they are…well, where does that leave my God? Or
> the big-G "God" of anybody's faith? Who is the
> god of whom, and why? And if my God and these
> other gods all exist in some kind of contin-
> uum…is there a winner, a loser?[1]

As we look deeper into the concept of worthiness in relation to Thor, some questions about his godhood naturally arise. In what sense are the Asgardians gods? Does Thor possess divinity? Should people worship him? And, most important, what is it that makes a god worthy? Although gods and godhood are not the main focus of this book, we should spend a little time thinking about these questions, which will be important for appreciating the concept of worthiness in Jason Aaron's run on the *Thor* comics.

Let's Talk about Godhood

Some of the best discussions of the Asgardians' godhood comes from religious figures on Earth, especially Catholic priests. The quote at the beginning of this chapter comes from a priest in Broxton, Oklahoma, who asks these questions during one of his sermons as Asgard hovers over the town, relocated there after a Ragnarok event. Another priest, Father Coza from New York, is saved by Thor and afterwards begins to question his faith, wondering if it had been misplaced all his life. Thor tries to provide comfort and assurance, telling him:

> There be many gods worshipped on this Earth, Father Coza, throughout this universe…They are given truth by the strength of faith and thus, through belief and prayer, all are made true…All spring from the same universal higher force. Your faith is not misplaced.[2]

Other priests are more hostile, especially when a sect of "Thorists" becomes popular around the world in response to the Asgardian's increasingly miraculous deeds. One tells Thor, "The Church is quite tolerant, but we find ourselves uncomfortable with one who proclaims himself a god and rallies the people to follow him." Thor responds, "I am a god. What else would I say?" But when the priest asserts, "There is only one true God," Thor says he doesn't care, has no interest in "your religion," and only wants to help. The priest explains the power of faith and says, "Your actions—your presence—undermine the people's faith in a higher divinity." Thor defends himself, claiming that "I ask no one to follow me in a religious sense," but the priest asks, "You claim godhood and have brought 'heaven' to earth. What else can you expect them to do? You contradict the beliefs of every established religion there is!" He adds later that "you offer the masses simple solutions to complex problems, dazzle them with seeming miracles. It is an affront to God and His word!"[3] Soon thereafter, Thor tries to bring a deceased girl back to life, and a priest flatly tells him, "Your work is an affront to my God. I believe you to be an evil of unparalleled proportion."[4]

As we see above, Thor often tries to avoid direct comparisons with the gods of the major Earth religions, especially the God of Christianity. When yet another priest asks him questions similar to the ones posed by his brother in Broxton—basically, "who are you?"—Thor puts him off, again and again, for years. Finally, as the priest lies on his deathbed, Thor offers an answer:

> I am not proof of anything but the complexity of creation. Whatever answers you may personally seek I suspect you are about to find them. The question is the same for me as it is for you: Who am I and why am I here? The answer remains the same as it ever was: Ask me tomorrow.[5]

The first part of his answer can be interpreted as Thor acknowledging that he is not the same kind of god as the priest's God, distinguishing between small-g and large-G, as the Broxton priest put it.

This is consistent with the way the various cosmic beings in the Marvel Universe are "ranked," as seen in a double-page spread titled "Relative Strengths and Comparisons" in the 1989 *Thor Annual*.[6] Thor himself introduces the topic, telling the reader:

> I am Thor, Prince of Asgard, and long ago the Norsemen did worship me and my kind as gods. 'Tis true that we Asgardians have powers far greater than those of the people of your world, Midgard. Yet there are beings in this cosmos whose might dwarfs even that of the God of Thunder!

He starts with a "powerless" Asgardian (Volstagg) and moves up the power scale to himself and his Greek analogue, Hercules, and then their fathers and patriarchs of the gods, Odin (whose power "exceeds that of all other Asgardians combined") and Zeus.[7] More powerful even are the "cosmic beings," such as Galactus, the Beyonder, and the Celestials, until we reach the truly godlike, including Eternity, who is the embodiment of the universe itself, and the Living Tribunal, who serves as judge throughout the multiverse.

At the end, Thor admits, "Even I, the son of one of the mightiest gods of all, find it impossible to conceive of such levels of power!" What is more revealing, though, is his final statement about the most powerful being of all, sometimes referred to in the comics as the One-Above-All: "And 'tis a humbling thought to consider how much greater still the power of the Creator of All Universes must be than all of his creations combined!" Here, again, Thor is acknowledging that he and his fellow Asgardians are not gods in the same sense as the all-powerful deities of most world religions, especially the creator-deities of the Christian, Jewish, and Islamic faiths—not even close.

There has even been some speculation in the comics—anticipating the position taken in the Marvel Cinematic Universe—that Asgardians are not gods in any meaningful sense. In one story, a soggy crowd blames Thor for the rain; he takes no credit but offers to stop it. When a bystander accuses him of thinking he's God, Thor replies that he is not a god in the theological sense, and begins to describe Asgardians as simply "a race of beings."[8] This is corroborated by a journalist who claims that a conversation between Thor and Nick Fury reveals that Asgardians are aliens, "a race whose technology has grown as advanced that it is indistinguishable from magic—even to them," building on the words of science fiction writer Arthur C. Clarke.[9] When Jane Foster and Donald Blake are chatting over lunch in their early days working together, they discuss how scientific theories of the origin of life are not so different from religious accounts, to which Don adds the Norse myths (curiously enough). Jane says, "It's like science, religion, and mythology all saying the same thing. Everything comes from one source," which Don silently acknowledges is true, but can't tell her how he knows without endangering his then-secret identity.[10]

Although he does claim a sort of godhood, Thor recognizes the distinction between small-g and big-G gods, as we've already seen. For instance, he rejects worship, arguing that it's more appropriate for gods with traditional divinity. The first time Thor encounters modern worshippers, or "Thor cultists," he disavows them, and when a television reporter tells him they are his followers and asks him to confirm his god-hood, he answers:

> Yes, but—no—I do not seek worship. That is long in the past…when the way of the warrior was once accepted. There are beings and powers far greater than myself, aye, even than All-Father Odin. These may be sought for spiritual enlightenment or moral instruction in this civilized world.[11]

After defeating the self-styled "Crusader," who was bent on eliminating the Asgardian "pagan god," Thor meets one of his cultists, who affirms her belief in him as her god (or God). Again, he rejects this form of worship, steering her toward more worthy gods and their mortal representatives: "Seek moral understanding and spiritual guidance, if you will, from those who are wise enough to instruct the mortals of this age in the name of today's gods! I am not a god fit for worship."[12] This statement not only affirms that Thor is a small-g, not large-G, god, and that he is very aware of this, but it also introduces the idea that some gods are not as worthy than others…and maybe not worthy at all.

Are Gods Worthy? Just Ask Gorr

> Forgive me, people of Earth, for the destruction I wrought while under Loki's spell! We gods of Asgard vow, with our supernatural powers, to repair all the damage done to your planet![13]

Thor's vow above, from a very early adventure, nicely captures the role and effect of the Asgardian gods in the affairs of modern Earth, where they are little worshipped and barely acknowledged (outside of the big Avenger with the hammer). In his exchanges with the priests recounted above, Thor makes clear that he serves and protects the people of Earth with no expectation of worship or tribute. At the same time, though, the

Asgardians cause no shortage of trouble on Earth, especially when their battles with the other realms—or with each other—lead to large-scale and widespread destruction there.[14] This leads us to wonder: What are these gods good for? What purpose do they serve, given that they're small-g gods, not the big-G, creator gods that people around the world worship and follow? And are they worthy, in a general sense (having little to do with a hammer)?

This question came to the fore at the beginning of Jason Aaron's run on the character when Thor becomes aware that someone was killing gods throughout the universe. After answering a prayer from the dry planet Indigarr for rain, Thor learns that they have no gods of their own, only "stories of gods from long ago who lived in a jeweled city high in the clouds."[15] When Thor investigates the gods' home, he finds them all brutally murdered, and he instantly recognizes the work of Gorr the God Butcher, whom he fought and defeated in his early, pre-hammer days, frustrating Gorr and reinforcing his mission to slay all gods. In the present day, Thor starts investigating other gods who have gone missing and finds countless ones, many dead for millennia, and thinks to himself, "What does it say about the gods in this universe that no one has ever even noticed or cared? What does it say about me?"[16]

We soon learn that Gorr is a creature from a nameless planet whose wife and daughters died of starvation, despite their continued faith in gods that never revealed themselves. Gorr began telling his fellow beings that their prayers were useless, that "the gods don't hear your prayers because there are no gods. There never were. No gods in the sky. No gods who made us. No gods watching over us. No gods who give a damn."[17] He was exiled from the community for his blasphemy, and as he wondered the desert of his world, two gods locked in battle fell from the sky, dying from their wounds. Not only did this reveal to Gorr that the gods do exist, but that they are flesh and blood, not immortal or divine as his people believed.[18] When one of them asked for help, Gorr grew enraged, asking where the gods were when his loved ones were begging for help while they died. Then he killed both gods with a mysterious weapon that formed in his hand from a black substance that came off one of the gods, and powered by the weapon—which we learn later is called All-Black the Necrosword—he flew into space to find more gods to kill.[19]

Gorr's origin story, as well as the larger story of his and Thor's battle in the first eleven issues of *Thor: God of Thunder* (January-October 2013), reveals much about gods in the Marvel Universe.[20] Despite their fantastic abilities, these gods are physical, flesh-and-blood beings, and because of this, they are not immortal—they may live a long time, but they can die, especially by violent ends. (They may come back from the dead, as Thor has on many an occasion, but in comic books, most people do eventually.) For all intents and purposes, they may be considered, as mentioned above, a "race of beings" with powers that grant them extraordinarily long lives. It doesn't take much to imagine normal humans seeing such beings and their miraculous powers and treating them as gods. (Just think about Simone Biles!)

Of course, not all powerful, near-immortal beings are considered beneficent, loving gods—just think of Galactus, the Devourer of Worlds. Somewhere along the line, we can assume a world's gods must have actually helped or protected the beings who worship or follow them. The inhabitants of Indigoor told stories of helpful gods, once upon a time, and even the beings of Gorr's world must have had reason, at one time, to believe in their gods. Even those who do not believe in gods of any sort can certainly understand why others do, given the mysterious nature and beauty of the universe.[21] In this sense, gods in the Marvel Universe acquire their purpose from helping lesser beings, often in exchange for their worship, admiration, and possibly tribute (even if just in terms of ale).

Wait a minute…this makes gods in the Marvel Universe sound a lot like superheroes! Perhaps not the powerless ones like Batman or Hawkeye, or those with a single power, like the Flash or most of the X-Men, but if we think about the mightiest superheroes, such as Superman, Wonder Woman, and of course Thor, we find they resemble this description of gods, at least in terms of what they do for people. Even if we assume gods serve an inspirational purpose, as moral exemplars demonstrating virtuous behavior, that still describes most superheroes (most of the time, at least). Many people have called superhero stories our modern mythology (especially since the runaway success of the Marvel movies), based on both their inspirational nature and their resemblance to Joseph Campbell's "hero's journey" that underlies many tales of myth.[22]

The only aspect of godhood discussed here that is missing in the case of superheroes is that of having followers and being worshipped. Superheroes may have fan clubs, but they don't have churches or cults formed in their name. We've seen that, in the present day, Thor is uncomfortable with this, but nonetheless he welcomed the worship of the Norse people "back in the day." There seems to be a loose exchange relationship between a Marvel Universe god and their followers that involves promises both ways: The god will protect the followers, and the followers will love and celebrate the god in return. That explains Gorr's frustration at his gods' neglect: His people suffered and died while they prayed to gods who entertained themselves far above the muck. Such gods do not deserve their followers' worship or admiration…in other words, they are unworthy.

Someone Begins to Doubt His Worthiness...

At the end of the first Gorr story, after Thor is joined in battle by his young, pre-hammer self and his future self, "King Thor," the God Butcher detonates his Godbomb, a device powerful enough to kill every god, everywhere in the universe and at every point throughout time. As gods begin to die, Thor fights Gorr inside the exploding bomb, eventually absorbing the Necrosword. As all the gods of the universe pray to him, Thor destroys the bomb and defeats Gorr, before collapsing in death himself, "for the ninth time that could be remembered," only to rise three days later. (No religious overtones there, nope.)[23]

Gorr may be down for now, but his influence will be seen in Thor's life for a long time to come. Earlier, Gorr told Thor that he'd figured out why he fights so hard, "why you try so desperately hard to seem noble. Because you see just how petty and useless your kind truly are. You know what I know. That gods have never created or cared for anything. Except themselves."[24] As Thor struggled inside the Godbomb, he couldn't stop thinking about what Gorr had been saying about the gods. "What if they really are better off without us...What if a godless age is what they deserve? What if Gorr...isn't a madman after all? Gods help us, what if he's..."[25] The Godbomb went off before he could finish his thought, but it's all too clear where he was going: What if Gorr is *right*, and gods *are* unworthy?

Thor's subsequent victory against Gorr would seem to validate *his* worth, at least, but Gorr's words still haunt him. After he "wakes up" from his three-day death, he says goodbye to his younger and older selves, the latter telling him to "be a better Thor than I was," and Thor responding, "Go be a king again, old man. And live to prove Gorr wrong." King Thor asks, "But what if he wasn't wrong?" to which Thor replies, optimistically, "Then we have even more work to do."[26] And he begins by returning to Indigarr and promising the beings there that they will never want for gods again, taking a first step to restoring the worth of gods to the mortals they serve.

Gorr's most devastating effect on Thor would come in *Original Sin*, a 2014 crossover event in which Uatu the Watcher is murdered, a crime that an assortment of heroes investigate while secrets that only Uatu knew from millennia of observing the events of the universe were released. The secret most relevant to Thor was that he has a sister, Angela, who lives in a tenth realm, Heven. On his quest to find her, Thor throws his hammer away during a battle, and when an enemy announces he is weaponless, he boasts, "Weaponless? Nay. As long as the son of Odin is worthy—that will never be."[27] Thor spoke too soon: At the end of the *Original Sin* story itself, on the surface of the moon, Nick Fury whispers something in Thor's ear that makes him drop Mjolnir, and try as he might he cannot pick it up again.[28] Thor finds himself unworthy, and it is not until several years later that we learn what Fury whispered in his ear.

"Gorr was right."[29]

****

After Gorr told Thor he had him figured out, he called him "the god who doubts."[30] This may seem like a taunt, but Gorr was on to something that will become more important as we progress through this book. For instance, in the midst of a battle with Malekith the Accursed, the narration calls Thor "a god who wondered every day if he was worthy without ever realizing…that was the very thing that made him so."[31] This statement is key to Thor's struggle to reclaim his worthiness, an adventure we will follow closely…but first, we have to meet the new Thor!

31

[1] *The Mighty Thor*, vol. 1, #1 (June 2011).

[2] *Thor*, vol. 1, #303 (January 1981).

[3] *Thor*, vol. 2, #64 (July 2003).

[4] *Thor*, vol. 2, #66 (September 2003).

[5] *Thor: Heaven & Earth* #3 (October 2011).

[6] *Thor Annual*, vol. 1, #14 (1989), "Relative Strengths and Comparisons." For more on the nature of gods and cosmic beings in the Marvel Universe, and how this relates to traditional theology and the philosophy of religion, see Adam Barkman, "'No Other Gods Before Me': God, Ontology, and Ethics in the Avengers' Universe," in Mark D. White (ed.), *The Avengers and Philosophy: Earths Mightiest Thinkers* (Hoboken, NJ: John Wiley & Sons, 2012), pp. 183–193, and Austin M. Freeman, "Gods Upon Gods: Hierarchies of Divinity in the Marvel Universe," in Gregory Stevenson (ed.), *Theology and the Marvel Universe* (Lanham, MD: Lexington Books/Fortress Academic, 2020), pp. 157–172.

[7] In the Marvel Universe, the Greek gods have roughly the same status as the Asgardians (or Norse gods).

[8] *Thor*, vol. 1, #481 (December 1994).

[9] *Thor*, vol. 1, #493 (December 1995). Clarke's "third law" first appeared in a letter in *Science* in 1968, available at https://science.sciencemag.org/content/159/3812/255.3.

[10] *Thor: Blood Oath* #1 (November 2005) and #6 (February 2006).

[11] *Thor*, vol. 1, #330 (April 1983).

[12] *Thor*, vol. 1, #331 (May 1983). In *Thor*, vol. 2, #51 (September 2002), Thor gradually becomes disappointed in humanity and eventually decides to rule them as an interventionist god, solving their problems for them and openly accepting worship in return, while still denying divinity (as the argument over the Thorists quoted above, from this period, shows). Things spiral out of control, and in *Thor*, vol. 2, #79 (July 2004), Thor—or "Lord Thor," as he becomes known—has to travel back in time to correct his mistake.

[13] *Journey into Mystery*, vol. 1, #94 (July 1963), "Thor and Loki Attack the Human Race!"

[14] The largest and most recent instance is the War of the Realms, which will be discussed later in this book.

[15] *Thor: God of Thunder* #1 (January 2013).

[16] *Thor: God of Thunder* #3 (February 2013).

[17] *Thor: God of Thunder* #6 (May 2013). (All events in this paragraph are from this issue.)

[18] As Gorr told the young Thor after capturing him: "You're meat, just like the rest of us, little god. Meat and bone and blood and innards" (*Thor: God of Thunder* #4, March 2013).

[19] In *Venom*, vol. 4, #4 (September 2018), it was revealed that the black substance that formed itself into the Necrosword was an early version of a symbiote, the most famous example of which formed Spider-Man's first black costume and later became Venom.

[20] Unless I say otherwise, when I refer to "gods" in this book from now on, I will mean small-g gods such as the Asgardians.

[21] On this theme, see William Irwin's essay "God Is a Question, Not an Answer," in *The New York Times*, March 26, 2016, at https://opinionator.blogs.nytimes.com/2016/03/26/god-is-a-question-not-an-answer/, and his book of the same name (Lanham, MD: Rowman & Littlefield, 2018).

[22] Joseph Campbell, *The Hero with a Thousand Faces* (New York: Pantheon, 1949). There is a wealth of interesting work exploring the links between superheroes and theology, such as Hutchinson (ed.), *Theology and the Marvel Universe*; B. J. Oropeza, *The Gospel According the Superheroes: Religion and Popular Culture*, 2nd ed. (Bern: Peter Lang, 2006); and legendary comics writer Grant Morrison's own *Supergods: What Masked Vigilantes, Miraculous Mutants, and a Sun God from Smallville Can Teach Us about Being Human* (New York: Random House, 2012).

[23] *Thor: God of Thunder* #11 (October 2013). This was an all-too-brief a summary of the story, which also involves King Thor's three granddaughters and Gorr's uncomfortable confrontation with his own godhood. It is a brilliant story in itself, and a great start to Aaron's epic run.

[24] *Thor: God of Thunder* #9 (August 2013).

[25] *Thor: God of Thunder* #10 (September 2013).

[26] *Thor: God of Thunder* #11.

[27] *Original Sin* #5.2 (September 2014).

[28] *Original Sin* #7 (October 2014); we also see him struggling to lift the hammer in *Thor: The God of Thunder* #25 (November 2014), the final issue of that title, before the next Thor is introduced in *Thor*, vol. 4, #1 (December 2014).

[29] *The Unworthy Thor* #5 (May 2017).

[30] *Thor: God of Thunder* #9.

[31] *Thor: God of Thunder* #17 (March 2014).

Chapter 3: Jane Foster, the Mighty Thor

Jane Foster is introduced in Thor's second story, after Donald Blake returns from Norway where he found the cane that transformed him into the God of Thunder. We see him tending to a patient with the assistance of a nurse, about whom he thinks, "Jane is so beautiful! If only I could tell her how much she means to me! But I daren't...for a girl so lovely would never marry a—a lame man!" Little does he know that she is also thinking of him: "I could care for him deeply, if only he would show some affection toward me...if even once he would take me in his arms and—and tell me cares!"[1]

Anyone reading this innocuous beginning would likely never guess that this run-of-the-mill superhero love interest, who will eventually (and predictably) fall for Thor too, only to wish her beloved Donald Blake were more like him, would someday wield the mighty Mjolnir herself. But in the five decades between when she first appeared and when she lifted that hammer, Jane Foster experiences a tremendous amount of growth as a character, becoming a doctor, a mother, and a valuable assistant to the Marvel superhero community (not just the Prince of Asgard). In the process, she displays a strength of character that leaves little doubt that she could be worthy—as far as Mjolnir is concerned, at least, and definitely Thor himself, if not his father.

To be fair, Jane Foster's true depth of character does not reveal itself right away, so Odin had reason to be skeptical in the early days. In flashback stories published later, she was shown to have more courage: In one such tale, Jane pleads with Thor while he is under the thrall of his brother Loki, striking out against the people of Earth and fighting its greatest heroes. After he breaks Loki's spell and defeats him, Thor tells Jane, "Thou wert truly the most valiant of all thy people…for thou stood thy ground with naught but the conviction of thine own heart."[2] In the original early appearances themselves, however, she was portrayed as the cooing female love interest for the male hero, lamentable but typical for comics at the time, and there were few signs that Jane Foster would eventually become the God of Thunder herself.[3]

After Thor and Jane first declare their love for each other (before Jane learns the truth about him and Donald Blake), the God of Thunder asks his father to make Jane immortal so they can marry, to which Odin responds, "To become an immortal, one must be proven to be noble, unselfish, fearless, and possessing virtues far in excess of those which the ordinary earthbound human possesses!"[4] These standards are similar to those for being judged worthy of wielding Mjolnir, which few immortals can do, so we can suspect that Odin was raising the bar a little too high for Thor's beloved; to his credit, though, he does not rule out the possibility that Jane can prove herself "worthy of immortality."

In the next issue, we see Jane's bravery and heroism when, after the villainous Mister Hyde abducts her and Blake, she complies with Hyde's commands, putting herself in danger to protect Blake, whom Hyde has tied up. Blake manages to escape and transform into Thor, but Jane believes Blake is still Hyde's captive, so when Thor drops his hammer, Jane hides it so the villain can escape, which she does, again, to protect Blake. But Odin does not see why she did these things, believing instead that Jane helped Hyde and betrayed Thor, so he declares that "she is not worthy" of immortality, despite her impressive display of courage for a mere mortal facing gods and supervillains.[5]

Despite Odin's disapproval, Jane and Thor stick together—itself a courageous act on her part!—and soon Thor reveals that he and Donald Blake are the same.[6] As explained in the first chapter, Odin relents and

35

endorses their marriage, but insists that Jane become an immortal. After he transforms her into a god, Odin makes her face the creature known only as the Unknown, which she survives only thanks to Thor, leading Odin to reject her as unworthy of godhood. Thor pleads her case by listing several of her virtues, different from his but no less admirable (and very ironic, given what lies in her future): "But—hear me, Father! She is no warrior! She is no Valkyrie born! She is but my beloved—gentle—and kind—and true!" Nonetheless, Jane agrees with Odin that she is not fit to be a god and begs to be returned to Earth, which the All-Father grants, erasing her memories of Asgard and transferring her love for Thor and Blake to a new man, Dr. Keith Kincaid, while re-introducing his son to Sif, his boyhood love.[7]

After that, Jane is mostly absent from the comics for nearly a decade (in our time), and when she does return, things get a little complicated. Thor discovers her in a hospital, dying from a mysterious, supernatural despair, and tries everything to revive her, including Asgardian treatments.[8] In the end, it is Sif, having come to accept Thor's love for Jane, who sacrifices her lifeforce to save the mortal.[9] From that point on, Jane begins to display many of Sif's valiant warrior characteristics, becoming bolder and more adventurous, leading Thor to exclaim, "Tho' a mortal born, thou has, truly, the courage of a goddess!"[10] Despite Jane's new-found godlike characteristics, Odin still does not approve of her and forbids Thor to be with her.[11] Before long, Jane strikes Sif's sword against a wall, similar to how Donald Blake changes into Thor, and she transforms into Sif—but unlike Blake and Thor, she finds this transformation cannot be reversed. The end result is that Thor is once again with Sif, who now carries within her the spirit of Jane Foster, who is seen occasionally and remains strong and heroic.[12] After another seven years, Sif tries to separate from Jane but finds the mortal is no longer part of her;

she and Thor find Jane's spirit and rescue her, after which she marries Keith, with whom she eventually has a son and later divorces.[13]

Jane's life is fairly normal for many years—which must have come as a huge relief after the events of the last paragraph—but more regularly displays courage, strength, and heroism. Refusing to be a "damsel in distress," on several occasions she tries to offer up her life to save Thor, including after her return to Earth following the failed attempt at godhood (as told later in a flashback).[14] Having been inspired by the early death of her mother to become a nurse so she would "never again be helpless to save someone I loved," Jane eventually becomes a doctor, working alongside Jake Olson, one of Thor's later mortal hosts, as well as Donald Blake when he returns to life following a Ragnarok event.[15] She also assists the broader Marvel superhero community, including during major catastrophes such as the battle with Onslaught and the Civil War.[16] On several occasions she travels to Asgard with Thor to confront Odin on his behalf—once with the support of Sif, her former soulmate (literally).[17]

The most recent development in Jane Foster's character—and the one that intersects most meaningfully with her upcoming stint as Thor—is her diagnosis of breast cancer, which we first learn about when the Odinson returns to Earth after his long battle with Gorr the God Butcher (as recounted in the last chapter). As he visits Jane in Broxton, Oklahoma, where she lives with her boyfriend Walter, Thor finds her smaller and thinner, with a bandanna on her head to cover her hair loss. She brings him up to date with her progress, including her surgery and chemotherapy, and she rejects his offer of Asgardian cures:

> We're not going down that road. Not ever again. No secret healing fountains. No Odin magic. You know that sort of thing always comes with a price. I'm a doctor. I'll fight this battle with plain old

Earth medicine. And if this is how I die, I will go down swinging, but on my own terms.[18]

When Thor tells her, "You are a brave woman, Jane Foster," she replies simply, "Nope. Just a regular woman. This is just something women do." Naturally, Thor is frustrated that there is nothing he can do to save Jane, but she does let him take her to the moon—specifically, the "blue area," which has air (and was once home to the Inhumans). There, she urges him to find a "nice Earth girl," and he says he's tried, but they all pale in comparison because "my last Earth girlfriend…was breathtaking." Jane did not know at this time that she would soon return to the moon, where there will be a hammer waiting for her…

If She Be Worthy

Soon thereafter, a catastrophic battle between Thor and Dario Agger, CEO of Roxxon Oil and occasional minotaur, leaves the town of Broxton completely destroyed (after the residents had all been evacuated). After his defeat, Agger stirs up sentiment against the Asgardians among the people of Earth, and Freyja tells her son Thor that Asgardia, which had hovered over Broxton since the destruction of Asgard in the "Siege," will be leaving Earth upon order of the Congress of Worlds (which governs all the realms).[19] Joined by other Asgardians, Thor offers his help to re-build Broxton and, before Asgardia departs, he carries his castle down to Earth to provide housing for its residents, telling them it is but "a small token of the debt you are owed…by Thor and all the gods." We see that the battle and its aftermath have taken its toll on Thor, who confides in Jane that, while he is staying on Earth, "I am not worthy of this world," yet another sign of the increasing doubts he has suffered since encountering Gorr.

More pivotal for Jane, Thor asks her to represent Earth on the Congress of Worlds, telling her that no one else on Earth has more experience dealing with Asgardians. He promises her this is not a ploy to lure her into accepting an Asgardian cure to her cancer, and assures her that the rainbow bridge Bifrost will be at her disposal to return to Earth for treatment.[20] Jane accepts, and leaves Earth on Asgardia beside Freyja.

It is from this new position on Asgardia that Jane hears the call from Earth's moon; as she tells Heimdall, "I have a voice in my head...and I won't insult you by lying about what it wants me to do. Just send me there. Before I come to my senses." After Heimdall uses the Bifrost to transport Jane to the moon, she approaches the hammer, muttering "there must always be a Thor," and as she lifts it from the ground its inscription changes to "if *she* be worthy."[21] The new Thor was introduced to the world in the first issue of a new volume of *Thor* in December 2014, her identity hidden from all—including the readers—until the eighth and final issue of that series the following July, before its relaunch as a new volume of *The Mighty Thor* after the universe-shattering *Secret Wars* event.[22]

Jane was not the first to try to lift Mjolnir after the Odinson dropped it, although she was the only one, mortal or god, deemed worthy. Before she picked it up, the Asgardians collected on the moon to watch the Odinson struggle to lift the hammer he long called his, only to have his father reinforce his feelings of inadequacy by saying, "What absurdity hath thou allowed to befall thee here, boy? How is it possible that the Prince of Asgard, the one true God of Thunder, the Odinson...has become...unworthy?"[23] Odin suspects evil magic, but after Freyja tells the collected gods what "the mortal they call the Captain of America" explained to her about recent events, her son simply mutters, "Whisper. All he did...was whisper." None of the other Asgardians can lift the hammer—even Volstagg, much to his surprise—and Freyja asks her beloved husband, "It was your enchantment, was it not, oh All-Father, that gave that thing the power to decide who was worthy?" But Odin himself cannot lift it, leading his wife to turn to their son, lying prone on the ground, and she tells him:

> It would appear the enchantment has grown beyond even the enchanter. Perhaps that is for the best…Worthiness should not be defined by the whims of magic weapons. Rise, my son, and let the hammer be damned. Rise and remember the hero that you are.

Freyja's maternal words raise an important question about worthiness: Who gets to decide whether someone is worthy?

Who Judges Worth…and Who *Should*?

Despite her development over the years, Jane was never really accepted by the All-Father, and when she became Thor herself, he was even more hostile toward her. One time, as they fought (Odin unaware of who this new Thor actually was), Jane reflected on their past interactions:

> There was a time I was in love with the god who once carried this hammer. And he was in love with me. We came awfully close to spending our lives together. There was only one reason we never did. His name is Odin. I was never good enough for the All-Father. Never worthy. A lot has changed since those days. So tell me, old man—am I worthy enough for you now?[24]

Whether or not she was worthy of Odin, Jane was definitely judged worthy by Mjolnir.

In the earliest stories, Mjolnir's "judgment" of worthiness reflected Odin's own: As one feature about the hammer reads, "no living being can lift Mjolnir unless he (or she) is someone who Odin, himself, would deem worthy of possessing the hammer!"[25] Certainly, Odin enchanted

40

the hammer, and served as the young Thor's guide to achieving worthiness, so it makes sense that Mjolnir would "follow" Odin's opinion of the worthiness of anyone who would wield it. Odin held the hammer in the past with no problem, but now he finds himself incapable of it, which can only mean two things: Either Odin no longer regards himself as worthy, which is highly unlikely, or the hammer now has judgment of its own that is separate from, and contrary to, that of its enchanter (as Freyja implied above).

And to be sure, Mjolnir did choose Jane and deemed her worthy, as the comics make very clear. As Jane first adjusts to being Thor, she speaks to the hammer—which she already suspects of being sentient—saying, "Mjolnir…let us hope you knew what you were doing, mallet, when you deemed me worthy of hefting you. For I am not putting you back down just yet."[26] Later, she tells the Odinson that "the hammer called to me," as she said to Heimdall before traveling to the moon to pick it up.[27] As she fights Malekith, Dario Agger, and Frost Giants—all in her first outing as Thor—Jane finds herself separated from Mjolnir, quickly losing power and strength, and wonders what the last God of Thunder would have done. "Thor would bellow and bluster and rage until they cut off his arms," she thinks to herself. "And then he would kick the hell out of them. The hammer chose me. That means I'll do nothing less. No matter the cost."[28]

After being reunited with the hammer, the new Thor meets her predecessor for the first time (in her current form), and she confirms to him Mjolnir's role in her being chosen. As their assembled foes watch in amusement, the Odinson demands that Jane "unhand my hammer," to which she responds, "I did not ask for this! The hammer chose me!"[29] As they struggle, both hand-to-hand and with thunder and lightning, the Odinson asks, "What makes you so worthy?! Who are you beneath that mask?!" The current Thor answers, defiantly, "I am the one holding the hammer! Who are you?!" The two struggle for Mjolnir before it takes off on its own and flies a twisting pattern to knock out the remaining Frost Giants, prompting the Odinson to admit, "In all our years together...in all our many battles...Mjolnir never flew like that for me." When he tries to summon the hammer back to him, it smacks him before returning to the new Thor. "You have brought new life to that hammer," says the Odinson. "Whoever you are...you are correct. It has chosen you." He presses her about her identity—suspecting at first that she is his mother—but she refuses, asking him to trust her. He says, "No. But it would appear the hammer trusts you. And I trust in the hammer." After defeating their foes, the Odinson proclaims, in front of the assembled Avengers and Asgardians who are helping with the aftermath of the bat-tle—and marveling at the new God of Thunder—that Jane is worthy whereas he is not, and that "she is Thor now."

If that isn't enough, Jane also tells the Warriors Three, who are among the Odinson's oldest and closest friends, the same thing on an early adventure together—a rite of passage for the new Thor if ever there was one! Fandral begins by daring to call her "Lady Thor," which she quickly corrects ("just Thor").[30] Next, he challenges her worthiness, ask-ing her, "What is it that makes you worthy to carry Mjolnir? I must say, I'm not too impressed as of yet," which she answers: "It's of no concern to me whether you are impressed or not. Mjolnir chose me. That's all I need to know." As they finish their adventures—with the new Thor ad-dressing several crises in a distinctly different way than the old one would have—they feast, drink, and relax, with Fandral acknowledging that "you're not like our Thor...but you *are* Thor. A new Thor, all your own. Forgive us for testing you. It was all in good fun!" She replies, "Oh, I know. I told you, I have no need to prove myself to you. Mjolnir knows I am worthy, and I know I am worthy."

This is an important statement from any Thor: Mjolnir knows Jane is worthy, *and Jane knows it too*. Throughout her run as Thor, Jane rarely shows the same doubts that plague the Odinson—which is understandable, given their different backgrounds, especially regarding their parents, and the fact that he is a god while she was born a mortal. Even though she ends up serving much less time as the God of Thunder than her predecessor did, Jane had served many years of her earlier life as a medical professional, performing feats of heroism with a stethoscope and scalpel for years before switching to a hammer. Far be it for me to make a joke about doctors and their "God complexes," but even if Jane does not have an oversized ego, it makes sense that these experiences granted her a firm level of self-confidence that continued through her time as Thor as well. (Not to mention that she performed both roles while fighting cancer!)

As we saw in the first chapter and will see even more in the next, the Odinson relies solely on the judgment of Mjolnir to confirm his worth, as he did ever since he was a young boy. Jane, however, never had to struggle for the approval of a hammer; the hammer called to her, and in doing so verified her knowledge of her own worthiness. She did not *need* the hammer to judge her worth, as the Odinson did, because she was not raised to question it. She does, however, encounter skepticism from others unlike anything her predecessor had ever known: Whereas he was born to the role and earned the hammer through centuries of labors and sacrifice, it seems to the Asgardians and even some of the other Marvel heroes that she either stole the hammer or cheated somehow to get it. Even after the Odinson himself endorsed her, deemed her worthy, and granted her his name, not all are convinced—especially the All-Father.

In her self-determination that she is worthy, Jane exemplifies a philosophical concept that goes by several names in different schools of thought, all of which describe a certain self-possession, setting your own path and living up to your own standards. Immanuel Kant, the chief deontological ethicist we met briefly in chapter 1, called it *autonomy*, "the property that the will has of being a law to itself."[31] In other words, autonomy is the ability to choose to do the right thing, which you determine for yourself using your rational faculties, despite external pressures and internal desires pushing you to do otherwise. Every hero, "super" or otherwise, who chooses the call of duty over their own happiness is exercising their autonomy: They are following the dictates of morality over whatever they would rather do instead, even at great sacrifice. (Some take this too far and deny themselves any personal life whatsoever, which is hardly virtuous in the sense of finding the golden mean between selfishness and selflessness, although we often call such behavior heroic.) More important for current purposes, because only *you* can know the motivation behind your choices—and even then not perfectly—it is up to *you* to judge whether you have lived up to the standard you set for yourself and to determine the true nature of your moral character or worthiness.[32]

In the school of philosophy known as *existentialism*, the concept of *authenticity* serves much the same purpose as Kant's autonomy. A central theme in existentialist writing, especially that of Jean-Paul Sartre, is self-determination, which is both a right and responsibility of every person: It is up to *you*, in the spirit of radical freedom, to decide who you are going to be, given your material conditions (or *facticity*), and then to hold yourself to that ideal.[33] Whereas Kant was more concerned in his ethics about people resisting their selfish and base impulses to follow the moral law, the existentialists focused on resisting influences from outside, especially informal pressure from other people. They held that every person has an obligation to be authentic to their own vision of who they want to be—and, as with Kantian autonomy, to judge to what extent they live up to that.

More generally, we can talk about this type of self-actualization and judgment in terms of *integrity*, one meaning of which refers to managing and balancing the different aspects of your moral character to create an internally consistent self.[34] A person who maintains their integrity always seems like the same person to outsiders, even when confronting a variety of situations and decisions, despite the moral complexities churning within them. Captain America is the epitome of integrity in the Marvel Universe, always making hard choices based on a bedrock moral code and holding himself to the same high standard.[35] The Odinson's adopted brother, Loki, may be the perfect counterexample to integrity: His very nature as a trickster god relies on being unpredictable. (However, if unpredictability is his nature and he remains true to it, that may endow him with an integrity of his very own, although it will be very difficult for anybody else to tell!)

Although by all accounts Jane seems to be a fine example of autonomy, authenticity, or integrity, the Odinson falls short, at least as far as assessing his own worth is concerned. To be sure, given his relatively simplistic moral code based on a handful of warrior virtues, he can certainly be said to possess integrity in his choices and action. When it comes to judging his own worth, however, he trusts too much in Mjolnir, while all too quickly losing faith in his own worthiness and his assessment of it.[36] In the coming chapters, we will see him come to appreciate a more elaborate understanding of worthiness than he learned as a child, but he still tends to rely too much on the hammer to verify it for him.

Jane, to her credit, is proud to be judged worthy by Mjolnir, but does not rely on it to validate her worth. Whereas Odin drilled its enchantment and its demands into his son from an early age, Freyja warns Jane against relying on the hammer's judgment, telling her early, "That hammer is the greatest trouble of all. It is a fickle mistress that makes fools of even the gods." She continues:

> Do not just be worthy of the hammer. You are not the first to wield it, and no matter your fate, you will not be the last. Be worthy of the name. Long after every hammer in creation has crumbled to dust, the name of Thor will echo still. That is the true honor you bear. That is the burden you must carry.[37]

In urging Jane to live up to the name Thor rather than the whims of a magic mallet, Freyja is trusting her to determine for herself what that name means and then hold herself to that self-determined standard—which corresponds to what I described above, whether we call it autonomy, authenticity, or integrity.

What Makes Jane Worthy? Just Ask Mjolnir

Even though Jane knows full well she is worthy, Mjolnir still needs to make that judgment to enable her to wield it. But first, we need to address the issue of whether or not Mjolnir is sentient.

We saw that Jane suspected its sentience soon after first picking it up, even telling the Odinson and Heimdall that it called out to her. There are several other early signs: As the new Thor fights Odin in space, she thinks to herself, "If I didn't know better…I'd swear I could hear Mjolnir laughing. Magic hammers must have a sick sense of humor."[38] Also, the hammer obeys her commands, such as when she asks it to find the Roxxon base.[39] Most striking, Mjolnir actually changes shape to impersonate Jane Foster after Thor catches a magic bullet that was meant for Dario Agger.[40] After "Jane" walks through the Bifrost with her doctor's bag, she removes the bullet, allowing Thor to see through her eyes while Mjolnir operates. This was all to preserve Thor's secret identity in front of nosy S.H.I.E.L.D. investigators who were convinced she was Jane Foster, but due to Mjolnir's ruse, they were dissuaded: "A puny little thing like that. Jane Foster is no Goddess of Thunder."[41] After they leave, Jane reveals her dual identity to Roz Solomon, the environmentalist S.H.I.E.L.D. agent who is also the Odinson's current love interest, wanting to show Roz the respect the other Thor took so long to give Jane. Roz asks Jane if Mjolnir is alive, and Jane answers, "That...is a very good question."[42]

We soon learn that Mjolnir is not simply a hammer forged by the dwarves of Nidavellir out of Uru metal and enchanted by the All-Father. It also contains the God Tempest,

> a cosmic thunderstorm the size of a galaxy, one that had been raging since the beginning of time, but it was more than that as well. The worst of its wrath was reserved only for those who truly deserved it, it was said. A storm that passed judgment. Almost as if...as if it had a mind of its own. A sentient super storm.[43]

When the God Tempest came to Asgard, Odin fought it for many days, eventually defeating it and trapping it into the hunk of Uru metal gifted to him by the dwarves, whom he then asked to forge it into a weapon. Odin named it "Mjolnir the thunder weapon," but found it unruly, describing it like a wild stallion, "too unbridled...too wild and untamed for even the gods," so he placed the enchantment on it that, as we saw in the first chapter, "would make it all but impossible for anyone else to lift it."[44] (Or so he thought.)

So why did Mjolnir, and the God Tempest trapped within it, deem Jane Foster worthy of wielding it and thereby earning the power and name of Thor? We have seen that Jane has always been courageous and heroic, in her interactions with Thor and the other Marvel heroes, but most importantly in her lifelong devotion to helping others as a nurse and a doctor, most recently while battling cancer. But we already saw that it took more than simple virtues for the Odinson to qualify as worthy: Before that happened, he had to show that he was willing to sacrifice his life for others without thinking.

We clearly see the willingness to sacrifice in Jane's case as well, not just in her actions as Thor—including making the ultimate sacrifice, as we'll see in a later chapter—but also in how she dealt with her cancer diagnosis and treatment while serving double duty as the God of Thunder. In the issue in which her identity is revealed to the readers, her narration reads: "I am Dr. Jane Foster. And I will not stop being the Mighty Thor. Even though it is killing me."[45] She elaborates in the next issue while she undergoes chemotherapy, describing how it feels and how the cancer has metastasized from her breast to other parts of her body. Her doctors don't understand why the chemo is not helping, but she knows full well: Every time she transforms into Thor, the chemicals are eliminated from her body but the cancer is not, "because cancer is just another part of me now. A part that keeps getting bigger...and is killing me a little bit more...each time I change back."[46]

Next, Jane asks herself the obvious question:

> So why change back at all? Believe me, I've asked myself that question many times over the last few months. But the answer is always the same. Not even the Mighty Thor is a match for every challenge. If I'm going to save everyone I know and love from the specter of war...then Jane Foster has a job to do as well.[47]

After she finishes her chemo, Jane returns to Asgard to meet with the Congress of Worlds to discuss the growing violence throughout the realms, as well as Odin's increasingly tyrannical behavior—a job she can perform only as Jane Foster, not the God of Thunder.[48]

Despite this ever-present concern, we see the instinctive and unreflective nature of this Thor's heroism and sacrifice when she tries to stop countless Roxxon bombs, sent by Malekith, falling toward Alfheim, the realm of the Light Elves. As she flies up to the bombs and begins to summon the thunder and lightning, she thinks to herself, "For the first time in forever, I'm not thinking at all about cancer or chemo or the problems of poor, frail Jane Foster. I'm one with the storm."[49] After destroying the bombs and reverting to her mortal form, Jane and Mjolnir both fall back to the surface of Alfheim, and she thinks, "If I'd never picked up the hammer, I wouldn't be in this mess. Instead I'd be in an infusion room somewhere, quietly treating my cancer. Getting better. But I regret nothing. Not a single thunderous second."[50] They both hit the ground with a thunderous "THOOM," and the smoke clears to reveal the Mighty Thor, with Mjolnir in her hand, to face Malekith once again (and again, and again).

After Thor caught the bullet meant for Agger and Mjolnir appeared as Jane Foster to remove it, the God of Thunder asks "Jane" for an explanation. Mjolnir speaks to her, saying it took an incredible amount of power to pull off the impersonation, and it doesn't know if it could do it again. When Thor tells the hammer she wants Roz Solomon to know the truth, it says, "If this is how you wish the day to end, then so be it, Thor. Truth be told…I would expect no less of you." As it transforms back into the famous Uru hammer, Mjolnir grants this Thor a favor it never did for her predecessor, revealing why it finds her worthy: "Your heart is stronger than even your thunder, my lady. That's what makes you worthy. That's why I chose you."[51]

The word "heart" is open to interpretation, to put it mildly. Given the context in which Mjolnir said it—Jane expressing her desire to share her secret with Roz Solomon—it could refer to a kindness and compassion that goes beyond the "mere" sacrifice and heroism the Odinson had to show to earn the hammer. Mentioned by the former Thor in defense of Jane when she "failed" at being a god in their early days together, these are sometimes regarded as more feminine virtues as described in psychologist and philosopher Carol Gilligan's 1982 book *In a Different Voice*, which argued that women and men have different ethical perspectives and frameworks, with women's based more on relationships and reflecting an ethics of care.[52] Separate from Gilligan's work, care ethics is now studied as another approach to moral philosophy, and is sometimes represented as a variant of virtue ethics focusing on specific character traits that are important to caring relationships.[53] These particular virtues are often associated more with women, whether for social or biological reasons, but obviously they can be possessed by men as well—which leads us to ask, naturally, whether the Odinson has them as well, or if Mjolnir recognizes different varieties of worthiness in different persons. Those questions, however, remain to be answered.

****

Of course, we may be reading too much into this, and by "heart" Mjolnir may simply mean the same strength of character, heroism, and sacrifice it recognizes in the Odinson...except that it no longer seems to find these in him at all.[54] In the next chapter, we'll return to the God Formerly Known as Thor and follow his new journey as he struggles with no longer being worthy, exploring what that means and how it feels, and how he might find a way back to worthiness again.

Interestingly, it is Jane Foster's closing words in the issue that revealed her identity to readers that may offer a clue as to what the Odinson must learn to be once again worthy of Mjolnir:

> The world needs a Thor. That's all that really matters. We need a god who understands what it means to be humbled. To be mortal. A god who knows how precious life is. How delicate. A god who

struggles every day to live a worthy life. Who suffers so that no one else will have to. A god who loves the Earth enough to die for it.[55]

Here we see familiar themes of sacrifice and humility, as well as the imperative to "live a worthy life," reminiscent of Aristotle's "the good life" (as described in the first chapter), plus a new concept: always striving to be worthy, which we will explore in the next chapter.

Most important, perhaps, is mortality and the appreciation of life it grants—which, at the danger of giving the All-Father too much credit, may have been part of his purpose in sending Thor to Earth in the form of Donald Blake in the first place. We will explore all of these themes in the chapters to come, as the Odinson fights to reclaim his worthiness and Jane tries to maintain her precarious mortality while facing the demands of being the Mighty Thor.

[1] *Journey into Mystery*, vol. 1, #84 (September 1962), "The Mighty Thor vs. the Executioner." Jane's last name is given here as Nelson; four issues later, the next time her last name is mentioned, it is Foster. (I'm sure there's a Marvel No-Prize in the offing for anyone who can explain that.)

[2] *Thor: First Thunder* #5 (March 2011).

[3] Well, maybe one: In *What If?*, vol. 1, #10 (August 1978), an alternate timeline is shown in which Jane Foster, not Donald Blake, finds a cane in Norway that transforms her into the Mighty Thor (or, as she calls herself, "Thordis"). (I doubt many who read this story in 1978 would have imagined Jane becoming Thor for real in 2014!)

[4] *Journey into Mystery*, vol. 1, #99 (December 1963), "The Mysterious Mister Hyde!"

[5] *Journey into Mystery*, vol. 1, #100 (January 1964), "The Master Plan of Mr. Hyde!"

[6] *Journey into Mystery*, vol. 1, #124 (January 1966), "The Grandeur and the Glory!"

[7] *Thor*, vol. 1, #136 (January 1967), "To Become an Immortal!" In *Thor*, vol. 1, #415 (March 1990), it is revealed that Kincaid was the model that Odin used to create Donald Blake to be Thor's mortal self.

[8] *Thor*, vol. 1, #231 (January 1975).

[9] *Thor*, vol. 1, #236 (June 1975).

[10] *Thor*, vol. 1, #241 (November 1975).

[11] *Thor*, vol. 1, #242 (December 1975).

[12] *Thor*, vol. 1, #249-250 (July-August 1976). After they are temporarily separated, Sif reflects on the experience, thinking, "They stripped away my Asgardian persona…and would have done the same with Jane Foster—eventually bringing about the death of the form we share—had not her own natural strength and courage carried her to safety" (*Thor Annual*, vol. 1, #9, 1981).

[13] *Thor*, vol. 1, #334-335 (August-September 1983) and #336 (October 1983), "Of Gods and Men."

[14] *Thor*, vol. 1, #475 (June 1994); *Thor*, vol. 1, #279 (January 1979).

[15] We learn she is a doctor in *Thor*, vol. 2, #1 (July 1998), after which she interacts with Jake Olson regularly, eventually learning he is also the God of Thunder. In *Thor*, vol. 3, #8 (June 2008), Donald Blake finds her working in the oncology department in a New York City hospital, and they go into practice together in Broxton, Oklahoma, in *Thor*, vol. 3, #615 (November 2010). The inspiration for her medical career was revealed in *Thor*, vol. 4, #8 (July 2015).

[16] Jane helped during the Onslaught episode in *Thor*, vol. 1, #502 (September 1996), and aided the resistance against superhero registration in *Civil War* #2 (August 2006). She appeared in a number of other Marvel titles in the late 1990s and early 2000s after her reintroduction as a doctor in *Thor*, vol. 2, #1.

[17] *Thor*, vol. 2, #21 (March 2000); *Thor Annual 2000*, vol. 2 (2000), "Final Confrontation"; *Thor*, vol. 2, #39 (September 2001).

[18] *Thor: God of Thunder* #12 (October 2013). (All the events of this paragraph are drawn from this issue.)

[19] *Thor: God of Thunder* #24 (September 2014); all the events in this paragraph and the next, unless otherwise noted, are in this issue. (Asgard was destroyed by the Sentry on the orders of Norman Osborn in *Siege* #3, May 2010.)

[20] Or to see her boyfriend Walter, but Jane tells him they broke up. (I know you were wondering.)

[21] *The Mighty Thor*, vol. 2, #705 (May 2018), shown in flashback; the scene on the moon was also shown contemporaneously in *Thor*, vol. 4, #1 (December 2014) without revealing Jane's identity.

[22] *Thor*, vol. 4, #1; *Thor*, vol. 4, #8 (July 2015). See the Reading Guide at the end of this book for more on the many volumes and titles of the Thor comics over the years, especially during the Aaron run.

[23] *Thor*, vol. 4, #1 (from which all in this paragraph is drawn). Freyja is the lone Asgardian who does not try to lift the hammer, casting it a wistful glance as the Asgardians leave the moon, making her a prime candidate for the identity of the new Thor—until the two meet in *Thor*, vol. 4, #5 (April 2015). As she watches the new Thor fly away after a brief chat, Freyja mutters to herself, "Should have picked the damn thing up when I had the chance..." (Note she doesn't say she should have "tried" to pick it up.)

[24] *The Mighty Thor*, vol. 2, #5 (May 2016).

[25] *Thor*, vol. 1, #400 (February 1989), "I...This Hammer! (Or, If You Knew Uru Like We Know Uru!)."

[26] *Thor*, vol. 4, #2 (January 2015).

[27] *Thor*, vol. 4, #4 (March 2015).

[28] *Thor*, vol. 4, #3 (February 2015).

[29] *Thor*, vol. 4, #4, from which all the events in this paragraph are drawn.

30 *Thor Annual*, vol. 4, #1 (April 2015), untitled second story; in *Thor*, vol. 4, #4, Spider-Man suggested Thunder-Woman, Thorita, and Lady Hammer Pants (but not to her face). On the same theme, *Thor*, vol. 4, #5 features an exchange between Jane and two of her predecessor's frequent foes, the Absorbing Man and Titania. The former blames the "damn feminists" for taking away "one of the last manly dudes left"—a not-so-subtle jab at the reaction from a small but vocal segment of the fandom to the introduction of a female Thor—while the latter is impressed, asking, "Thor? Thor's a woman now? Like the for-real Thor? She ain't called She-Thor or Lady Thunderstrike or nothing like that?" Eventually she stands down, "out of respect for what you're doing. Can't have been easy for you."

31 Immanuel Kant, *Grounding for the Metaphysics of Morals* (trans. James W. Ellington, Indianapolis, IN: Hackett Publishing Company, 1785/1993), p. 441. Roger J. Sullivan discusses Kant's use of the word "autonomy" and how it differs from other meanings in *An Introduction to Kant's Ethics* (Cambridge: Cambridge University Press, 1994), pp. 125–128. For an application of Kantian autonomy to a number of contemporary moral issues, see Thomas E. Hill, Jr., *Autonomy and Self-Respect* (Cambridge: Cambridge University Press, 1991).

32 On how Kantian ethics relates to moral character, see Sullivan, *An Introduction to Kant's Ethics*, ch. 8; there will be more on this topic in the next chapter.

33 For more on Sartre and other existentialists regarding authenticity, see Somogy Varga and Charles Guignon's entry on the topic at *The Stanford Encyclopedia of Philosophy* (Spring 2020 Edition), Edward N. Zalta (ed.), at https://plato.stanford.edu/archives/spr2020/entries/authenticity/. On existentialism in general, a great introduction is Sarah Bakewell's *At the Existentialist Café: Freedom, Being, and Apricot Cocktails* (New York: Other Press, 2016).

34 For more on the sense of integrity, see Lynne McFall, "Integrity," *Ethics* 98 (1987): 5–20. A wider look at the concept is provided by Damian Cox, Marguerite La Caze, and Michael Levine, in "Integrity," *The Stanford Encyclopedia of Philosophy* (Spring 2017 Edition), Edward N. Zalta (ed.), at https://plato.stanford.edu/archives/spr2017/entries/integrity/.

35 For more on Cap and integrity, see chapter 4 in my book *The Virtues of Captain America: Modern-Day Lessons on Character from a World War II Superhero* (Hoboken, NJ: John Wiley & Sons, 2014).

36 And his father, of course, but that's a subject for another book—ideally by someone with psychological training!

37 *Thor*, vol. 4, #5.

38 *The Mighty Thor*, vol. 2, #5.

[39] *The Mighty Thor*, vol. 2, #9 (September 2016).

[40] *The Mighty Thor*, vol. 2, #10 (October 2016).

[41] *The Mighty Thor*, vol. 2, #11 (November 2016). When they interrogated her and demanded she tell them who the new Thor is "or else," she just laughed, telling them, "I'm dying of cancer, you jackasses. What exactly do you think you've got that you can threaten me with?" (*The Mighty Thor*, vol. 2, #8, August 2016).

[42] Ibid. In *Thor*, vol. 5, #9 (March 2019), Roz tells Jane that she tried to lift the hammer herself before Jane picked it up for the first time, but couldn't. "I'm not worthy, Jane. I'm not you." The Odinson apparently disagreed: Before the new Thor's identity was revealed, he accuses her of being Roz, only seconds before Roz showed up to accuse Jane of spoiling her operation against Agger and Roxxon (*Thor*, vol. 4, #8, July 2015).

[43] *The Mighty Thor*, vol. 2, #12 (December 2016). The idea of the God Tempest having been trapped in Mjolnir recalls the many times Thor summoned "the storm" through the hammer, even in space, such as when he uses it to defeat Galactus in *Thor*, vol. 1, #161 (February 1969). (It does not seem to be related, however, to the Godstorm introduced in *Thor: Godstorm* #1, November 2001.)

[44] *The Mighty Thor*, vol. 2, #12.

[45] *Thor*, vol. 4, #8.

[46] *The Mighty Thor*, vol. 2, #1 (January 2016). In an interesting example of parallelism, when the Odinson first fights alongside the new Thor and watches her wield the hammer that was his for centuries, he listens to the hammer's "song of thunder" that he has "heard countless times before. But never quite like this," and his thoughts turn inward: "With every rumble of thunder…With every roaring note of the hammer's song…I die. I die a little more inside" (*Thor*, vol. 4, #4). (This also foreshadows the Odinson's issues with his own self-worth, which we explore in the next chapter.)

[47] Ibid.

[48] I should also note that throughout her time as Thor, the mortal Jane Foster is depicted, usually by artist Russell Dauterman, realistically as a woman battling breast cancer, while still helping to protect the world from evil. The grateful letters from readers—either fighting cancer themselves, caring for loved ones with cancer, or having lost someone to the horrible disease—attest to how powerful this portrayal was and how much it meant to so many people. (See, for example, the letters in *The Mighty Thor*, vol. 2, #21, September 2017, and *The Mighty Thor: At the Gates of Valhalla* #1, July 2018.)

[49] *The Mighty Thor*, vol. 2, #3 (March 2016).

[50] *The Mighty Thor*, vol. 2, #4 (April 2016).

[51] *The Mighty Thor*, vol. 2, #11.

[52] Carol Gilligan, *In a Different Voice: Psychological Theory and Women's Development*, rev. ed. (Cambridge, MA: Harvard University Press, 2016).

[53] See, for instance, Nel Noddings, *Caring: A Feminine Approach to Ethics and Moral Education*, 2nd ed. (Berkeley, CA: University of California Press, 2003), and Virgina Held, *The Ethics of Care: Personal, Political, and Global* (Oxford: Oxford University Press, 2007). On the feminist nature of care ethics, see section 2.2 of Kathryn Norlock, "Feminist Ethics," *The Stanford Encyclopedia of Philosophy* (Summer 2019 Edition), Edward N. Zalta (ed.), at https://plato.stanford.edu/archives/sum2019/entries/feminism-ethics/.

[54] Freyja apparently had the same idea when she told the young Thor, still trying to become worthy of Mjolnir, "Thor. My beloved son. Look at me. Look at your mother, Freyja, and hear my words as if they were thunder. No hammer in all the heavens can make you a better god. Only the heart that beats in your chest can do that" (*The Unworthy Thor* #4, April 2017).

[55] *Thor*, vol. 4, #8.

Chapter 4: The Odinson, the Unworthy Thor

As we learned at the end of chapter 2, Nick Fury whispers in Thor Odinson's ear that "Gorr was right" about the unworthiness of the gods, which makes the Asgardian drop his mighty Mjolnir.[1] After untold years of struggling as a young god-prince to earn the right to wield the mystic hammer, and then continuing to prove himself worthy in countless adventures throughout the Ten Realms, it takes just one whisper to render the Odinson unworthy. He soon finds another Thor holding Mjolnir, and after initially challenging her for both the hammer and the name, he endorses her for both. After telling him that the hammer chose her, Jane refuses the name, calling him Thor instead, to which he replies, "Do not call me by that name. I am not worthy of it." After his mother Freyja objects, he continues, "I am still the Prince of Asgard. I am still the Odinson. But she is Thor now."[2]

The Odinson has started to accept that he is unworthy—according to Mjolnir's judgment, at least—and from this point he begins a journey of exploration into what this means for him, as well as how to reclaim his worth, his name, and his hammer. He does not immediately embrace this new path, though: When he presses the all-seeing Heimdall for anything he knows about the new Thor's identity and "why she is worthy when I am not," the guardian of the Bifrost tells him to "focus less on her worthiness and more on your own."[3] He next visits mortal Jane in the Asgardian Hall of Medicine after she collapsed during a meeting of the Congress of Worlds. As she receives chemotherapy (still refusing Asgardian treatments), she jokes with the Odinson that "I survived trolls, super villains, Civil Wars, your brother, your dad. After all that, you think I'm gonna let some little lump in my breast be the thing that takes me down?" He answers, sullenly: "Sometimes a whisper can fell even a god. Be not prideful, Jane Foster. Not at a time like this."[4] After a subsequent adventure together, the new Thor tells her predecessor that "in my eyes, no one is more worthy than the Odinson," to which he replies, "Hmph. Tell that to the hammer."[5]

The Odinson then leaves Asgard, Earth, and the *Thor* comics themselves for a while, reappearing in the 2017 miniseries *The Unworthy Thor*, our main focus in this chapter. In the opening of the first issue, he remembers his glory days of feats and battles, but soon acknowledges that "I am not that god anymore. That god was worthy. I am the Odinson. The lost scion of Asgard. The unworthy. The god formerly known as Thor."[6] In these five issues, the Odinson struggles to overcome his unworthiness—in part by seeking out other hammers that he hopes will grant him the validation he craves—and eventually comes to terms with it and understands the role it will play in his becoming worthy once again.

The Self-Loathing Thor

For the Odinson, being unworthy does not simply mean being turned away by Mjolnir: Because he has relied on the hammer's judgment all these years for affirmation, its rejection hurts him profoundly. When he first tells the Warriors Three about Fury's whisper—after a long night of drinking—they try to carry him to bed. Fandral tells him he's had enough, to which the Odinson replies, "Enough? You underestimate the pains of unworthiness, Fandral, my friend. It will be enough…once I can hear no more whispers."[7] Later, the Odinson reflects on the fact that he's been sleepless since becoming unworthy, "I haven't slept, because I've been afraid of what I'd see if I closed my eyes. I was right to be afraid," because he dreams of a whispering Mjolnir bearing down on his chest and crushing it, followed by Gorr reminding him of his own self-doubt.[8]

Unlike Jane, who knew her own value and worth long before the hammer chose her, the Odinson never developed this self-assurance, always striving to win the approval of Mjolnir—and to some extent, by proxy, his father, although that would always be much more difficult to achieve. As a result, the Unworthy Thor lapsed into an intense period of self-loathing that far surpassed any rejection he suffered from his hammer or father. After being taken captive by the Collector, one of the Elders of the Universe, and forced to fight for his freedom and the chance to wield a different Mjolnir—originating on Earth-1610, otherwise known as the Ultimate Universe, most of which was destroyed in the 2015 *Secret Wars* event—the Odinson affirms his unworthiness and thinks to himself, "now I spend my mornings not flying but fighting. And failing. And fighting again."[9] He's much more direct about his feelings about himself after he fights Ulik and his fellow trolls, only to watch them escape: "Gods, I hate trolls. Almost as much as I hate…myself."[10] When he once again meets Nick Fury—now in the form of the Unseen, condemned by the Watchers to observe the universe without interfering—the Odinson challenges him, "what did I have for breakfast?" Fury responds, "alcoholic beverages, and self-loathing." In response, the Odinson mutters, "lucky guess," but there was no luck involved: Fury doesn't need the sight of a Watcher to know how low the former Thor's self-image has fallen.[11]

There are many reasons a person may become self-loathing, many of them having to do with childhood trauma, especially at the hands (literally or metaphorically) of a caregiver.[12] It is clear that the All-Father was very hard on his son, but perhaps the worst thing he did was encourage him to try to live up to the expectations of a hammer that he never meant anyone to wield. Once, when Thor was young, Odin saw him trying to lift Mjolnir and scolded him, "What in the name of Bor do you think you're doing, boy? Unhand that weapon at once! That hammer was never meant for the likes of you, Thor!"[13] On top of setting his son up to fail, Odin also demanded that Thor live up to his father's expectations and standards rather than develop his own. We do not have to deny that Odin has good intentions and was raising Thor to be a worthy god and future king of Asgard, but as with many royal children throughout history who were destined from birth to play a predetermined role in society, Thor had very little chance to develop his own personality and moral character aside from what was demanded of him—at least without rebelling against his father's authority, which he did by clinging to Earth and loving a mortal, Jane Foster.

The Odinson does not feel unworthy only in terms of Mjolnir's standards as he may understand them, specifically the traditional warrior virtues of courage, heroism, and sacrifice for others. Once people begin to doubt their value or worth in one part of their lives, it is often difficult to maintain confidence in other parts, especially to the extent those aspects of their lives are connected. (Someone who feels inadequate in their job is more likely to feel inadequate as a provider at home, for example.) Like Jane's cancer, the Odinson's self-loathing spreads from one part of his life—that governed by the approval of Mjolnir—to the rest, further eroding his belief in himself and taking him even farther from the redemption he hopes for.

We see this when, after fighting the trolls and talking with the Unseen, the Odinson is visited by Beta Ray Bill, the Korbinite who was the first person after Thor to wield Mjolnir. Now considered by the Odinson to be "brothers in thunder," they originally met as enemies, and when Bill defeated Thor and separated him from Mjolnir long enough for Thor to revert to Donald Blake, Bill picked up Don's cane and was transformed into a Thor-like version of himself.[14] When Odin summoned

Thor back to Asgard, it was Beta Ray Bill who appeared, and after the All-Father demanded to know what he had done to his son, Bill threw Mjolnir at him—and Odin caught it, signaling that, at one time, Mjolnir did judge its creator worthy.[15] Odin called his son back and explained the nature of the enchantment to Bill, who nonetheless refused to relinquish a weapon that could enable him to protect his people after the core of their galaxy exploded. Odin struggled with the fact that "both you and my son have a claim of Mjolnir, the hammer, by your worthiness and your need," and ordered them to fight for the right to wield it.[16] After a hearty fight, Bill was victorious, but both warriors nearly died from the battle; after Bill told Odin he refused to take the hammer that was meant for Thor, Odin rewarded him with his own enchanted hammer, Stormbreaker, that granted him the same powers as Thor.[17]

In the present day, Beta Ray Bill offers Stormbreaker to the Unworthy Thor, who refuses it in turn, while thinking to himself, "now his friendship is clearly yet another thing…of which I am no longer worthy."[18] Rather than acknowledge his friend's offer as a sign of his respect and admiration, it shames the Odinson and reinforces his feelings of inadequacy, despite there being nothing to suggest that he has lost any claim to this friendship. It is the fact that the Odinson no longer feels he is worthy at all, because Mjolnir has judged him so in terms of possessing the power of Thor, that makes him reject any sign that others hold him in high regard; he dismisses their positive comments as pity or flattery because, in his mind, they could not possibly be sincere.

This general feeling of inadequacy also extends to the Odinson's relationship with S.H.I.E.L.D. agent Rosalind Solomon, which had only just begun before the whisper destroyed what was left of his self-confidence. The first time they see each other after his disappearance, she tells him she looked for him when he was gone and was disappointed he never made contact. The Odinson drops his head and says, "Of late, there are many things of which I've found myself unworthy. You were one." With this, he extends his self-loathing to his romantic partner as he did to his old friend Beta Ray Bill, finding her continued affection in his diminished state to be unjustified. Of course, those who care for a self-loathing person maintain their right to make up their minds about who is worthy of their care, but the intended recipient tries to deny them even that. So when Roz answers, "You could've let me be the judge of that," he responds that "it hurts too much for you to see me like this," rejecting her affection before she can reject him, which would be the direct affirmation of his unworthiness that he fears even more.[19]

The Odinson's self-loathing goes as far as to deny he was *ever* worthy, despite all evidence to the contrary. At what is perhaps his lowest point, he thinks to himself, "I never deserved to be worthy in the first place. Never did. Never will. Worthiness was a cruel dream. All I am truly worthy of now…is misery."[20] This comment reinforces that such intense and prolonged feelings of inadequacy are often associated with clinical depression, displaying similar features of *dichotomous* or *black-and-white thinking*, such as when the Odinson regards himself as either worthy or unworthy, completely and always, and *exaggerated* or *catastrophic thinking*, in which positive feedback (such as praise) is dismissed and negative feedback (such as criticism) is magnified, which only serves to reinforce feelings of inadequacy and leads to cascades of self-loathing.[21] We have seen this when the Odinson extends his feelings of inadequacy from the hammer's judgment of him as a god and hero to the validity of his relationships (and implicitly the judgments of his friends and loved ones), and ultimately to his self as a whole. Once a person is convinced they are inadequate in some way, they are often set on a downward path in which the feelings of self-loathing deepen and spread throughout their life until it is all-encompassing…and that is where we find the Odinson in his "Unworthy Thor" phase.

On the Road Back to Worthiness…

How does a self-loathing person, such as the Odinson, find their way out of this downward spiral? There is no quick and easy answer, but somehow they have to rediscover their faith in their self-worth, and learn to rely on their own judgment on who they are rather than relying on someone (or something) else. In the terms we used in the last chapter, they have to be *autonomous* or *authentic*, setting standards for their own moral character and then holding themselves to them, rather than letting someone else do it for them. By doing this, a person can reclaim their own integrity based on their self-determined standards, or in the terms of existentialism, create themselves as authentic persons.

This is a difficult lesson for the Odinson to learn—and one could argue he really never takes it to heart—but many of his close friends and family try to reinforce it. As we saw before, Freyja told him when he was young and struggling to earn the right to wield Mjolnir that "no hammer in all the heavens can make you a better god. Only the heart that beats in your chest can do that."[22] After he loses the hammer, Jane Foster visits his quarters in Asgardia in her mortal form to check on him, and he tells her that he is "quite busy. Busy being useless and unworthy." She says, "As someone who has loved you for a very long time, believe me when I say…the hammer doesn't make the man. You are so much more than just a chunk of Uru." But the Odinson dismisses her words, replying that it's "easy for you to say, Jane Foster. You've never held it," unaware that she very much has (although she has not struggled with issues of worth as he does).[23] In the present day, when the Collector orders him to explain how to lift the Ultimate Universe Mjolnir—for which he stole the entirety of old Asgard, on which it landed when its original universe was destroyed—the Odinson says that "you're asking the wrong Thor" and tells him about the enchantment. When the Collector threatens to kill a young boy to force the Odinson to tell him what he wants to know, the former Thor shouts, "I can't even lift my own Mjolnir! I can't make my-self worthy, let alone you!"[24] The irony here is that he actually can "make himself worthy," if only he can believe in his own worthiness again.

During the short run of *The Unworthy Thor*, the Odinson does start to see this, but in a more complex way that reveals the hidden depths of what worthiness can mean, especially to a hammer named Mjolnir. As he rallies Beta Ray Bill to fight the Collector and his guards to get the alternate-universe hammer, he says:

> They think me weak because I am unworthy. I am still a god and more than a god. I am Asgardian-born. The blood-son of Odin. The lord of the storm and the raging thunder. And I'll be damned if I need a hammer in order to raise some Hel. But this day I will claim one nonetheless. No matter how much blood I must wade through. So swears the Unworthy Thor.[25]

Even though he calls himself unworthy as far as Mjolnir is concerned, his other words suggest that he still acknowledges some self-worth in another way: as a god, born in the most powerful of the Asgardian gods, and one who can still command the lightning and the thunder. At the same time, he finishes by proclaiming himself "the Unworthy Thor" as he starts to embrace his new status and come to terms with it—which, as we will see, is essential to reclaiming his worthiness, albeit in a para-doxical manner.

In the next issue, he affirms his quest for worthiness in another grand speech while he fights for the other Mjolnir. He thinks to himself:

> I have faced countless fearsome battles over the years. Fighting alongside gods and Avengers. Taking on giants and cosmic con-querors and beings beyond even an immortal's comprehension. But today I fight a battle unlike any other in all my many eons of

smiting and thundering. Today I fight to be whole again. To be the god I was always destined to be. Today I fight to be worthy.[26]

After he battles his way to the mysterious hammer, he reaches down to grip its hilt, thinking again:

> A whisper. That was all it took. A whisper I still cannot unhear. And worse yet…cannot refute. A whisper. A whisper was all it took to bring me down. To rise again, I need to be stronger than whispers. Stronger than my enemies. Stronger than unworthiness. And I need one other thing. I need a hammer.[27]

To be "stronger than unworthiness" is not necessarily the same as being worthy; instead, it may mean accepting his unworthiness but not letting it control him, in the same way heroes accept their fears but use courage to overcome them.

The Odinson's words at the end of *The Unworthy Thor* suggest just this. After touching the Ultimate Universe Mjolnir, he realizes it is not his hammer to wield, and he and Beta Ray Bill—with the help of Thori, the Hel-Hound and self-professed "murder dog" whom the Odinson found trapped in the Collector's museum—restore the original Asgard, with the alternate Mjolnir still embedded in its crust, to its original location in space.[28] Bill asks the Odinson if he could have lifted the hammer and if he "believe[s] in his worthiness again," and the Odinson responds, simply, "no god is worthy." When Bill asks what he means, his brother-in-arms reveals to him—and, for the first time, to the readers—that Fury's fateful whisper was "Gorr was right." As the Odinson elaborates,

> Gods…are vain and vengeful creatures. Always have been. The mortals who've worshipped us for centuries…would all be better off without us. We gods do not deserve their love. No matter how much we fight to fool ourselves. We are all unworthy.[29]

With this, the Odinson shows that he acknowledges his unworthiness, not as a lesser god among better ones, but as a god who is unworthy by nature. Bill replies that, even with a hammer, the Odinson fights none-theless, and "every day you give your blood, your tears, your immortal soul…to prove Gorr wrong. The gods may not be worthy, but you are no mere god, my friend. You're Thor."[30]

…a Paradox Emerges

In describing his friend's never-ending efforts to be a better god, Beta Ray Bill gets to the heart of worthiness as far as Mjolnir is concerned: *It's the struggle to be worthy that makes one so.* As it turns out, the Odinson knew this the whole time—or, at least, he did once. In a flashback to his early days when he was romantically involved with Jane Foster, they are lying in bed in Asgard, and Jane finds him staring at Mjolnir, as he does every morning, "like you're afraid to touch it." He admits that he may be, and when Jane says that he's fought "the most terrifying monsters imaginable. Including your father," and asks why he'd be afraid of his own hammer, Thor explains:

> It took me years to be worthy of Mjolnir. Many years and many dragons and ultimately a particularly unpleasant showdown with…Well, 'tis a story for another time. Yet worthiness is not an absolute condition. It is something for which even a god must never stop striving. I fear this hammer, because every morning when I wake…I never know if I will be able to lift it again…until I do.[31]

Jane embraces him and says, "and that's exactly why you'll always be worthy"…at least until he forgets and has to relearn this important les-son.

The idea that an ongoing struggle to be worthy is essential to being worthy—especially if you begin with the awareness that you might not yet be worthy—echoes several concepts from different areas of philosophy. For example, recall Immanuel Kant's concept of *autonomy*, the ability to resist external pressures and internal desires and instead do the right thing according to the moral law. Although all persons possess the ability to make decisions autonomously, some of us are better at it, or do it more reliably, than others. This capacity for autonomy, which Kant called "virtue," can also be called a person's strength of character or will, which Kant said must be developed and cultivated much as one does with a virtuous character trait: "the way to acquire [strength] is to enhance the moral incentive (the thought of the law), both by contemplating the dignity of the pure rational law in us and by practicing virtue."[32]

But we're not done once we've achieved a reasonable level of strength of character or will, because nobody is perfect—no mortal, at least, and no god in the small-g category. According to Kant, only the will of a truly divine God is flawless because such a being has no material interests to tempt it.[33] The rest of us must keep up the effort to remain virtuous and moral: As Kant said about strength of will, "if it is not rising, [it] is unavoidably sinking."[34] We can see that, not only is the ongoing struggle to remain strong of character necessary to be virtuous, but maintaining this effort, in the face of never-ending temptation, is virtuous in itself—and in Thor's case, it is an essential part of being worthy.

The importance of acknowledging one's unworthiness while struggling to be worthy is reminiscent of other concepts from the last chapter, particularly those from Eastern philosophies such as Taoism and Buddhism. Many are familiar with the *kōan* of Zen Buddhism, such as "imagine the sound of one hand clapping," philosophical puzzles that inspire us to think about concepts in different ways, similar to how the Western philosopher René Descartes encouraged us to be skeptical about the nature of reality, knowledge, and our own minds.[35] It's not difficult to find the same apparent paradoxes in common language, such as the logical contradiction in the simple phrase "I am lying": If I'm lying when I say this, that means I'm actually telling the truth, which means I'm actually lying...and so on.

There is a similar contradiction in claiming to have certain virtues that are based on not claiming them, such as modesty or humility. Can someone sincerely claim to be humble? It seems not, because humility involves *not* trumpeting your virtues, including humility.

Worthiness is a lot like humility in that being too confident of it, or being too comfortable in always possessing it, actually makes you less worthy. Ideally, a person would reach the "golden mean," like Jane does: Her sense of worthiness was always confident while not arrogant, and tempered by her awareness of her mortal fallibility. For the Odinson, however, it is more difficult to maintain the golden mean, having been born the God of Thunder and presumptive heir to the throne of Asgard, so it may be easier for him to maintain worthiness by thinking himself unworthy and constantly trying to improve.

Also, the struggle to be worthy in Mjolnir's judgment should be routine or unthinking, recalling the Taoist concept of *wei wu wei* that we discussed earlier: "action through inaction," or achieving something by *not* striving for it. In the last chapter we saw that, with things like happiness and love, we must put whatever goal we're working toward out of our minds and instead focus on doing things that will lead to it, thereby achieving them indirectly and without counterproductive effort. This is the lesson the Odinson has to learn—or, to be more accurate, learn again, because the unthinking or automatic part of sacrifice and heroism was always part of the criteria for being worthy of Mjolnir. When young Thor reacted to the threats to Sif and Freyja by immediately putting his life on the line for theirs, he forgot about "trying" to be worthy—he simply did something that *made* him worthy.

When Heimdall recommended the Odinson focus less on the new Thor's worthiness and more on his own, he was only half right, because the Odinson needed to forget about his own worthiness altogether and recapture what made him worthy in the first place: unthinking heroic sacrifice. He must continually struggle to be worthy, while not thinking about the goal of worthiness itself. In other words, he should pursue worthiness by not pursuing it—in other words, by remembering *wei wu wei*.

****

However, he's not quite there yet. At the end of *The Unworthy Thor*, the Odinson remains unworthy, although he has begun to see the way back. In the final chapter of this book, we will explore how he finally manages to reclaim his worthiness by denying it, while Jane Foster proves once and for all why she was always worthy...even if it kills her.

[1] *Original Sin* #7 (October 2014).

[2] *Thor*, vol. 4, #4 (March 2015).

[3] *Thor*, vol. 4, #6 (May 2015).

[4] Ibid. Afterwards, she implores him not to call himself the Odinson, because "you're so much more than just your father's child." (She suggests "Lord Thunder Britches" instead.) Later, she tells him that "'son of Odin' sounds more like an insult than a name" (*The Unworthy Thor* #2, April 2017).

[5] *Thor*, vol. 4, #8 (July 2015).

[6] *The Unworthy Thor* #1 (January 2017).

[7] *Thor*, vol. 4, #5 (April 2015).

[8] *The Unworthy Thor* #2 (February 2017).

[9] *The Unworthy Thor* #1.

[10] Ibid.

[11] Ibid.

[12] For example, see Nerisa Banaj and Clelia Pellicano, "Childhood Trauma and Stigma," in Gianfranco Spalletta, Delfina Janiri, Federica Piras, and Gabriele Sani (eds), *Childhood Trauma in Mental Disorders: A Comprehensive Approach* (Berlin: Springer, 2020), pp. 413–430.

[13] *The Unworthy Thor* #3 (March 2017).

[14] In the now-classic *Thor*, vol. 1, #337 (November 1983).

[15] *Thor*, vol. 1, #338 (December 1983).

[16] Ibid.

[17] *Thor*, vol. 1, #339 (January 1984).

[18] *The Unworthy Thor* #2.

[19] *The Mighty Thor*, vol. 2, #23 (November 2017).

[20] *The Unworthy Thor* #3.

[21] See Aaron T. Beck, *Depression: Causes and Treatment* (Philadelphia: University of Pennsylvania Press, 1972), which contributed to the development of *cognitive behavioral therapy*, an approach to treating clinical depression based on identifying distorted modes of thinking such as the ones described above.

[22] *The Unworthy Thor* #4.

[23] Ibid.

[24] *The Unworthy Thor* #2.

[25] *The Unworthy Thor* #3.

[26] *The Unworthy Thor* #4.

[27] Ibid.

[28] Thori was introduced in *Journey into Mystery*, vol. 1, #632 (February 2012), and is a very good boy (at least when he's not murdering).

[29] *The Unworthy Thor* #5 (May 2017).

[30] Ibid.

[31] *The Unworthy Thor* #4.

[32] Immanuel Kant, *The Metaphysics of Morals* (trans. and ed. Mary Gregor, Cambridge: Cambridge University Press, 1797/1996), p. 397.

[33] Immanuel Kant, *Grounding for the Metaphysics of Morals* (trans. James W. Ellington, Indianapolis, IN: Hackett Publishing Company, 1785/1993), p. 414.

[34] Kant, *Metaphysics of Morals*, p. 409.

[35] René Descartes, *Meditations of First Philosophy* (trans. Donald A. Cress, Indianapolis, IN: Hackett Publishing, 1641/1993).

Chapter 5: The Two Thors

The Fate of Jane Foster

> Jane Foster feels most alive when she is fighting. When there is something in front of her she can punch or throttle. For she cannot throttle the cancer that is ravaging her human form. And recently she has begun to wonder…if she should bother having a human form at all. Why not live the life of a god forevermore? Why not hold the hammer until the end of time? The more she thinks those thoughts, the tighter the Goddess of Thunder grips her Mjolnir. And the more Jane Foster slips away.[1]

As Jane Foster approaches her greatest test as the Mighty Thor, a central theme in her ongoing story is the conflict between her mortal self and the godhood she has been granted by Mjolnir. This issue is further complicated, not only by the cancer that is ravaging her human self, but her lifelong ambivalence towards gods in general.

For example, recall the scene from Jane and the Odinson's early relationship, told in the last chapter, in which he was hesitant to lift his hammer for fear that he might not be able to. After Jane tells him "that's exactly why you'll always be worthy," she elaborates:

> I grew up in a home devoted to science. I never believed in any god. Not even when I was nine, watching my mother die of cancer. I'm still not sure what I believe, even after all the wonders I've seen here in Asgard and beyond. Maybe your father did create the first

humans from a couple of ash trees. Or maybe you're all just aliens who live a really long time. All I know for sure is…you're the kind of god I've always wanted to believe in, Thor.[2]

Jane now lies in a hospital bed, trying to resist the siren call of the hammer so she can continue her mortal battle against cancer, and she remembers her mother in a similar bed, telling Jane that she had never been religious and therefore didn't raise Jane in any faith. She later comes to regret it, though, and wishes she'd left Jane with "something to believe in that's greater than us." She finishes by asking her daughter to "find a god to believe in, Jane. Find one who's worthy of you, my beautiful daughter." In the current day, Jane reconsiders what she said to the Odinson all those years ago and thinks to herself, "I could never find a god to believe in. Instead the gods found me."[3]

At times, Jane expresses outright hostility toward the gods, levying the same grievances that we heard from Gorr the God Butcher in chapter 2. After her husband Keith and son Jimmy were killed in a car accident, the Odinson came to her to offer the condolences of all of Asgard. Rather than accepting them, she railed at him, demanding to know "where were you, Thor? Where was Odin or Sif or Hercules? There are more of you out there than I can count. Always meddling in our lives when it suits you. Where were any of you tonight?"[4] After Jane becomes the Mighty Thor herself, she faces off against the gods of the Shi'ar Empire who told her they would "teach you what it truly means to be a god." Incredulous and offended, Jane shouts back about a woman she held in her arms mere days ago as she died of cancer, despite praying "to all the gods." She repeats her argument about how many gods there are, all of them so boastful "of their own majesty and almightiness," but in the end she doesn't know which heaven the woman is in because "no god bothered to listen or care."[5]

At the same time, however, Jane suggests a more reciprocal relationship between mortals and their gods. In a much earlier story, after being saved by Thor, Jane tells a "suddenly" reappeared Donald Blake, "I wonder if Thor realizes how much we appreciate having someone like him in the heavens…looking out after us mere mortals? I wonder if we mere mortals will ever understand what it must cost to love us that much?"[6] She may have been a bit lovestruck when she said that, but she says something similar many years later: After she demands to know where the gods were when her son and husband died, she walks away from the Odinson, muttering, "'Find a god to believe in.' I tried, Mother, I did. But I don't think they believe in us. And I don't blame them."[7] Even though it's not clear exactly what Jane thinks mortals owe gods for their love and protection—without even considering the gods' own failures in that regard, as expressed by her at other times, or the distinction between "small-g" and "big-G" gods—this suggests that the separation between mortal and god may not be so clear-cut for Jane Foster, even before she embodies that duality herself and faces the temptation of giving up her mortal life for one as the Goddess of Thunder.

After stepping down from the Congress of Worlds—and nominating Roz Solomon to take her place—Jane finally tells the Odinson her secret (off-panel, unfortunately).[8] Soon afterwards, she takes the Bifrost to Old Asgard, where the Odinson and his Hel-Hound Thori stand guard over the Ultimate Universe Mjolnir. After he rants for a bit regarding the double blow of her secrecy and then her revelation, Jane confides to him that she's afraid. The Odinson assumes she means she's afraid of lifting Mjolnir, as he once was, but she corrects him, explaining that "I'm not afraid of lifting the hammer. I'm afraid that the next time I do…I'll never put it down again." She goes on:

> I have stage four cancer. It started in my breast. Spread to my lymph nodes. My liver. I haven't been fit to practice medicine for

many months. That job in the Congress of Worlds I said I hated...I did it because it gave me purpose. It gave Jane Foster a purpose. Without it...what reason do I have to hang onto this...this rapidly failing human flesh? Either Jane Foster dies in a hospital bed, or I kill her myself. By forgetting she ever existed. And staying the Goddess of Thunder. Forever.[9]

She finishes by saying, "That's why I'm afraid, Odinson. I'm afraid that no matter what I do next, I'm losing my...," but she is interrupted by her Mjolnir crashing down to Asgard—ironically, because we can safely assume she was going to say her humanity, in which she fails to see much continuing value compared to the good she does with that very hammer as the Mighty Thor.

Before she can lift it, however, Jane collapses, and the Odinson takes her to the Hall of Medicine and Spiritual Healing on Asgardia. There, they argue about using magic to cure Jane's cancer once and for all, while Mjolnir hovers nearby. The Odinson orders it away, blaming it for Jane's suffering, but she says weakly, "there is trouble in the realms," before touching it, transforming into Thor, and disappearing. The exposition on the next page reads:

"There is trouble in the realms," the hammer whispers. And Jane Foster answers without a second thought. That is why she is worthy to be Thor, the Goddess of Thunder. And why she will soon be dead.[10]

This short statement both confirms Jane's worthiness and concisely explains its three standard elements: heroism, in addressing the "trouble in the realms"; sacrifice, in that she is pushing her mortal self closer to death every time she transforms; and unthinking action, in that she "answers without a second thought." In addition, the importance of her humanity and her "heart" is emphasized when she faces an enraged Volstagg, mourning the death of five child dwarves in his care and transformed by the Ultimate Universe Mjolnir into the "War Thor."[11] After fighting him in vain as Thor, she drops her hammer and confronts her dear friend as mortal Jane Foster, calming him down by appealing to the gentle soul she knows resides within him.[12]

Jane's appreciation of her mortal form is a fleeting impulse, though. "There are so many realms in peril. And so few thunder gods," she thinks to herself as she rushes from one world to another, saving people and fighting wrongdoers. She wonders when she last slept, "but there isn't time to be anything other than Thor. Not as long as the War of the Realms is still raging."[13] The Odinson seeks her out and demands she return to Earth for her cancer treatment, making it clear he'll fight her if he must. When she says he'd be fighting on the side of their enemies, he replies: "No—of life. For my mortal friend, Jane Foster. Do you still remember her, Goddess of Thunder?" When Jane says she doesn't have time, the Odinson says, "that is the hammer talking. Not the doctor who wields it." She says she's not afraid to die if necessary to save the Ten Realms, but he implores her, "then don't be afraid to live." He praises her accomplishments, calls her "one Hel of a Thor," and lists the foes she has faced—including "my bastard back-stabbing brother" and "my Uru-headed father"—then says, "Now face this. For the world needs more than just a Thor. It needs you, Jane Foster. All of you."

Jane agrees to return home for treatment, but not before confronting the Odinson's Uru-headed father in her mortal form and once again proving the value of her humanity. She calls out the All-Father for ignoring the trouble in the Ten Realms and letting his brother Cul rule Asgard like a tyrant.[14] As you can imagine, Odin does not take well to a mortal challenging his authority, much less his son's former girlfriend from Earth. (He doesn't know yet that she's also the current Thorn in his side.) He threatens to deal with Jane more directly when Freyja suddenly appears, having recently recovered from a near-fatal wound, and agrees with Jane—and, implicitly, Gorr—when she says that "the realms deserve better gods. We…we are all unworthy." She tells the collected Asgardians that Jane's words inspire her, that they must prove themselves worthy as gods by protecting the Ten Realms, and that "we must be worthy…of her. Of the bold and valiant Lady Jane of Midgard." She summons Jane to her side, but the mortal has once again collapsed.

Jane finally submits to treatment back on Earth, surrounded by friends who try to convince her to fight the cancer as hard as she fights for others across the realms. Roz Solomon tells her that "the world needs you around for as long as it can get you, Doc," and Sam Wilson—former Captain America and current Falcon, as well as Jane's fellow Avenger and current love interest—leaves her a phone message to check in and says he hopes she's not forgetting "that there's more to life than just thunder." And Doctor Strange says that "being the world's greatest Thor…doesn't have to also make you the world's worst doctor! Or an even worse patient."[15] Together with the Odinson, they hold an intervention in Jane's hospital room, with Strange telling her that the cancer may have progressed too far by this point to be stopped, even by the most aggressive treatments, and that one more transformation into Thor will surely be her last, and she will never be able to return to mortal form.

Jane doesn't look at him, but instead stares at Mjolnir hovering outside her window, telling her that Mangog, one of the greatest threats any Asgardian has ever faced, has returned. The Odinson commands the hammer to leave Jane alone, but she starts to get out of bed nonetheless, saying, "I'm sorry, my friends. I truly am. But there's trouble in Asgardia. Thor is needed." As Jane approaches the hammer, Doctor Strange stresses again that her mortal body cannot withstand another transformation: "If you change into Thor…even one more time…there will be no coming back. Jane Foster will die." The Odinson and Sam try to stop her, but Roz says, "It's her life. She's gotta make this decision herself."

This time, Jane rejects Mjolnir's pleas, instead charging the others to fight on her behalf and then returning to her bed. Before long, though, she overhears Roz frantically talking on the phone about the worsening situation in the Ten Realms. Jane takes one last look at her medical chart, saying to herself, "I would've beaten you, you little cancerous sons of bitches," then removes the intravenous needle from her arm and takes hold of Mjolnir.[16] Next time we see her, Thor is locked in a brutal fight with Mangog, who has already destroyed Asgardia and the Bifrost. After she traps him in gold melted down from a statue of Odin, the All-Father and Freyja warn her that Mangog is too strong, but Thor will not stop, imploring them to get the other gods to safety.

When the Odinson joins them, angry that Jane has ended her mortal life—and could very well end her immortal one—she is undeterred, remaining Hel-bent on redeeming the gods themselves as well as saving them: "We need gods we can believe in! Tell them that! Tell all of Asgard! Tell them it's time to earn the gift they've all been given!"[17]

In fact, when Mangog escapes and he and Thor renew their battle, they launch into their own discussion of gods and their worthiness. Mangog perceives that this Thor is not "merely" a god although she fights for them nonetheless, and he presses her on this, saying, "You've hated them, too. Deep in your heart, you know they deserve this. They deserve everything I bring to them!" She grants some of what he says, but cites the reciprocity she sees between gods and mortals: "Aye, I've hated the gods as much as anyone! Because I know they've failed us all when we needed them most! But they've saved us, too, even when we did not deserve it! And now is my chance to return the favor!" Mangog explains that her fight is futile, that "you could sacrifice yourself a thousand times and they would still never change," and asks her, "why would you die for the gods?" Thor thinks about all the important people in her life, mortals and gods alike, and answers, "I die for love, Mangog. You die for naught but hate. That is why you lose."

Thor throws Mangog into the sun—causing Odin to ask himself, "why didn't I think of that?"—but the monster soon returns. While he's weakened, she ties him up in chains "forged by the dwarves of Nidavellir to bind the monster-wolf Fenris until the day of Ragnarok" and attaches the end of the chain to Mjolnir. Her final words to Mangog are: "In the end…it was not a god. 'Twas a mortal. Named Jane. A woman who gave up everything in order to stop you. Remember that." Then she whispers to the hammer, "Fly true, my friend. Fly like the mighty storm you are," and sends it into the sun, with Mangog bound behind it, this time never to return.

At first, the Odinson is shocked and mortified that Thor "killed Mjolnir," but soon he realizes how she has condemned herself as well. She removes her helmet, assuring him she knows exactly what she's done, and continues to refuse Asgardian treatments. Instead, she touches his face, looks into his eyes, and kisses him as she transforms into mortal Jane Foster; then he carries her body down to the moon, where the rest of the Asgardians await them both.

Heimdall confirms, "she is gone. The Goddess of Thunder is dead."[18] Jane Foster, the Mighty Thor, sacrificed her life, without hesitation, to save the Asgardians and possibly the entire universe from Mangog. While the Asgardians share their shock, awe, and dismay at learning that Jane had been Thor all this time, her spirit arrives at the Gates of Valhalla, final resting place of noble warriors—when who should appear beside her but Odin. Initially angry at her for "stealing" Mjolnir and his son's name, as well as daring to challenge the All-Father, he comes to acknowledge that she beat Mangog when no one else could, and made the ultimate sacrifice to do so. Finally, he says, "Jane Foster of Midgard.

You have earned your place among the most venerated of fallen warriors. Your eternal reward awaits. Welcome to Valhalla. Mighty Thor."

Odin, the sensitive All-Father that he is, can tell something's wrong with Jane, and when he asks her what it is, she replies, "I wasn't ready to die." At the same time, back on the moon, Heimdall senses that the God Tempest, who once resided in Mjolnir, is now unleashed and very angry—as is the Odinson, who shouts into the sun, "Down here, you bastard cyclone! Show me why they call you the God Tempest!!!" He summons the storm to him and channels it into Jane's prone form, trying to restart her heart with cosmic thunder and lightning, but it is no use—at least not until Odin arrives, puts a hand on his tired son's shoulders, and tells him, "You cannot control the powers of the God Tempest. No one god ever could. But luckily for Lady Jane…there is more than one of us." Together, father and son command one final stormblast, and the woman at their feet awakens. Thanks to Thor, Odin, and the God Tempest, Jane Foster lives.

Passing the Name (If Not the Hammer)

This monumental issue ends with Jane and the Odinson walking together on Asgard, surveying the rebuilding efforts, while Jane assures her dear friend that she is back in treatment, with Freyja and Roz watching closely over her—and "without the hammer around." As soon as she says it, she realizes the effect this reminder has on its former owner, and tells the Odinson, "I wish there'd been another way." He replies, "It was a worthy death for Mjolnir. Together you saved the gods. You saved my beloved friend Jane Foster. It was a worthy death for the Mighty Thor."

But just as Jane was not ready to die at the Gates of Valhalla, she is not ready to see the name perish either, telling her dear friend, "Thor can't die, son of Odin. Not now. Not ever." The Odinson claims to be reconciled to it, though, still ceding all judgment of his worth to his lost hammer: "With Mjolnir no more, I will ever be the unworthy Prince of Asgard. I will make my peace with that. The age of Thor has ended." After Jane tells him that the War of the Realms still rages and the world still needs a protector, she hands him a pebble that, as he takes hold of it, pushes his hand nearly to the ground. She explains that it's a tiny piece of Mjolnir that she found on the moon, the only piece left that she's aware of. Rather than be happy, though, the Odinson only bemoans the fact that he can barely lift the pebble, which "tells me I could never lift the entire hammer. That I'm still not…" Not only does the hammer still not judge him worthy, but apparently he hasn't accepted unworthiness nearly as much as he claims.[19]

Jane tells him, "The hammer made me the thunderer. But not you. You did that yourself." She asks him to look at her, then continues:

> "There must always be a Thor." That's what I said right before I lifted Mjolnir and was transformed for the very first time. I was honored to carry that mantle for a while. Honored that you bestowed upon me your own name. But it's time you reclaimed who you are. There must always be a Thor. And now…once again…it must be you.

The Odinson stammers (mightily), and Jane finishes, "I showed you what I could be with that hammer in my hand. Now show me what you can be without it. Show us all."

As the two longtime friends embrace before parting, they leave each other with words that affirm their affection for each other and also, much as Jane did earlier, refute the strict dichotomy between gods and mortals. The Odinson says, "I love you, Jane Foster. You are more a god than I could ever be," and Jane replies, "and you've got more humanity than most humans I know. I love you, too. Thor."[20] This echoes something she told him when she, as Thor, met the young pre-hammer Odinson, thanks to the wonders of time travel: "'Tis not your divinity that will make you the god you are destined to become, young Thor. 'Tis your humanity. Never forget that."[21]

The Odinson's humanity, both a legacy from his birth-mother and the result of his living among mortals as one of them, will play an important role in the rest of his own story—which involves finishing his path back to worthiness, as well as many, many new hammers.

Thor Odinson Once Again…But Is He Worthy?

Even after he reclaims his name, the Odinson—sorry, I mean Thor—still struggles with issues of unworthiness and self-loathing. Unfortunately, this happens at the same time as the War of the Realms—Malekith's grand offensive, which has been building since he re-emerged after Thor's fight with Gorr the God Butcher—reaches fever pitch, dominating the final act of our story, both in the fifth volume of *Thor* and the *War of the Realms* miniseries. The details of the war itself, which draws in most of the heroes in the Marvel Universe, are less important to us than its effects on Thor himself and what he learns about worthiness in the process.

Still grieving the loss of Mjolnir, Thor has the master dwarves of Nidavellir make him a number of substitute hammers out of Uru metal, on which Odin places a mild enchantment to grant their wielder limited powers (such as flight), with no worthiness required.[22] This is fortunate, because while fighting his nephew, the giant wolf Fenris, in Hel, Thor indulges in some self-recrimination, repeating Gorr's pronouncement which he has now come to accept as fact:

> The realms are burning, and I cannot stop the war from raging. Like I couldn't stop Asgardia from exploding in the sun, along

with my hammer. The one I couldn't lift anymore anyway. No god is worthy, especially not me. The eons will roll by one after another until all the stars have grown cold, and I will still be there, mourning everyone I have ever loved but couldn't save.[23]

As he and Fenris plunge into a poisoned Hel-river, Thor expresses his continued self-loathing as he thinks to himself, "There is no place for you here on these shores, the waters whisper. The immortal Thor is unworthy of even dying."[24]

Thor has also not accepted that he must be the judge of his own worthiness, relying instead on the hammer as well as his friends and relatives—anybody but himself. While imprisoned with his sister Angela in Heven, he asks her if he is worthy. After they are free, she answers him:

> I would like to tell you yes. But I'm afraid I am too scarred to ever be the arbiter of such things. I am not worthy of calling you worthy, I suppose you could say. I can only tell you this: You are the beating heart of the realms, Thor Odinson. Not just for Asgard. For all of them, whether they want to admit it or not. Without you, the skies would be silent and Yggdrasil would be nothing but a gallows hung with dead worlds. So if you are not worthy, brother…then what the Hel hope do any of the rest of us have?[25]

Angela later recounts their exchange to Jane, Roz, and Freyja over coffee in New York, where they all share their concern over their beloved Thor as he threatens to exhaust himself trying to save the Ten Realms while struggling with his own self-doubt.

He has also not given up on his beloved hammer, which he still believes is his one true link to worthiness. According to Freyja's narration, every day her son dives into the sun, searching for "any last trace of his fallen comrade, his blessed Mjolnir. And more importantly, his own self-worth." She tells him, "No hammer is worth your suffering. I've been telling you that for years. Now you must finally listen, for all our sakes," but he doesn't hear her, instead pleading, "You don't understand, mother. You can't understand. What it means to me. How I need it." She tries to boost his confidence, arguing that he is "more than just a god. More than the Prince of Asgard. More than the mere offspring of an All-Father and Earth Mother," and more than enough to win the War of the Realms, "for you already wield your greatest weapon. Always have and always will. It's time you remembered what that is." After they both save people on Earth from disastrous weather caused by his unstable moods, Freyja thinks to herself what that weapon is: "the heart that beats inside his chest. Nothing in all the realms is stronger than the heart of Thor."[26] This echoes Mjolnir's explanation to Jane Foster about what ultimately made her worthy, suggesting that the Odinson possesses "heart" in the same general sense—at least in his mother's eyes.

After the War of the Realms reaches its climax, many Thors are brought into the fight, including Jane Foster, now cancer-free, who proclaims, "There must always be a Thor. And sometimes…there must even be more than one!" and picks up the Ultimate Universe Mjolnir to become Thor once again.[27] Joining her are two more Thors: King Thor, from the far future, and young Thor, who sees King Thor's Mjolnir and tries in vain to lift it, frustrated that he is still not worthy. King Thor warns his younger self to be careful not to fall in battle and endanger the versions of Thor to come, but when young Thor hears Freyja scream after Venom grabs her, he thinks to himself:

> Suddenly I no longer give a damn whether I die and take every other Thor along with me. My only thoughts are for the one parent who's always shown me love and compassion over the years…I think of her and I am moving instinctually, punching her monstrous attacker over and over. With all the power in my fists. Yet something…feels different somehow.[28]

That something is the fact that he's holding King Thor's Mjolnir high over his head, thanks to risking his life to rush to his mother's aide without thinking of the costs (as described in chapter 1). In that moment, this version of young Thor becomes worthy (although he will eventually return to his own time and continue working to earn the right to wield his own Mjolnir).

Unfortunately, the present-day Thor does not reclaim his worthiness so easily. After diving into the sun to find the world tree Yggdrasil, which has regrown from the ashes of the destroyed Asgardia, Thor impales himself on the tree, as Odin did centuries ago, to gain wisdom.[29] After he sacrifices one of his eyes for knowledge and gives up the pebble from his original Mjolnir, the tree explodes, shooting Thor back to Earth, with the realization of what he needs to win the war: more Thors. This is what led him to ask Reed Richards and Ben Grimm of the Fantastic Four to travel through time to gather his younger and older selves—Jane was just a pleasant surprise—to form "the storm of Thors." But that is not the only storm involved: Thor has also brought the God Tempest back with him from the sun, where it had been since restoring the fallen Jane Foster to life. He uses it to forge a new Mjolnir, its handle crafted from a piece of Yggdrasil, and bearing the new inscription: "Whoever holds this hammer, if *they* be worthy, shall possess the power of…Thor."[30]

But can Thor wield the new Mjolnir? Is he worthy once again? Malekith says no, but Thor lifts it anyway, revealing that he finally understands what it truly means to be…

> Worthy? Then I hope I never feel worthy again, for as long as I live. It's only the struggle that counts. "Gorr was right." But knowing that is what makes me strong. Not the hammers. Not the thunder. What I truly am, Malekith, now and forevermore…is the God of the Unworthy.[31]

Thor is now worthy precisely because he regards himself as unworthy, and therefore will never stop trying to become worthy. When he says, "it's only the struggle that counts," he means that being worthy is a process rather than an achievement. As we discussed in the last chapter, "worthiness through unworthiness" has the paradoxical feeling of a Zen *kōan* or the Taoist concept of *wei wu wei*, and also Immanuel Kant's position that one has to continually strive to be good to truly be good. Once Thor realizes these things and accepts the lifelong struggle to be worthy, he becomes worthy.

Even better, Thor now realizes that it is this knowledge, *his* knowledge, that makes him worthy, not the judgment of Mjolnir itself. He has internalized what Freyja and Jane have been telling him this entire time: that he must believe in his own worth, whatever that means to him. After Thor uses Mjolnir to defeat Malekith and end the War of the Realms, Jane tells him, "The hammer doesn't make the Thor. The Thor makes the hammer," to which he replies, "This time, quite literally." When she says, "I knew you'd remember that eventually, Odinson," he tells her, "I had a fine teacher, Lady Jane."[32] And he doesn't forget, even in his very, *very* old age: When young Thor asks King Thor why he didn't just give the current Thor his Mjolnir, the elder Thor answers, "It wasn't the hammer that was missing."[33]

[1] *Generations: The Unworthy Thor & The Mighty Thor* #1 (October 2017).

[2] *The Unworthy Thor* #4 (April 2017).

[3] *The Mighty Thor*, vol. 2, #704 (April 2018).

[4] Ibid.

[5] *The Mighty Thor*, vol. 2, #16 (April 2017).

[6] *Thor: First Thunder* #5 (March 2011).

[7] *The Mighty Thor*, vol. 2, #704.

[8] *The Mighty Thor*, vol. 2, #19 (July 2017).

[9] *The Mighty Thor*, vol. 2, #20 (August 2017).

[10] *The Mighty Thor*, vol. 2, #21 (September 2017).

[11] *The Mighty Thor*, vol. 2, #20.

[12] *The Mighty Thor*, vol. 2, #23 (November 2017). Earlier in this issue, while they're fighting—Jane holding both hammers in her hands—Volstagg questions her willingness to give her all to a war. She shouts back, "You think I cannot understand war? Try battling cancer!!!"

[13] *The Mighty Thor*, vol. 2, #702 (February 2018); all the events in this paragraph and the next are from this issue.

[14] This is the same Cul who died while killing the Odinson in *Fear Itself* #7 (December 2011).

[15] *The Mighty Thor*, vol. 2, #703 (March 2018); all the events in this paragraph and the next are from this issue.

[16] *The Mighty Thor*, vol. 2, #704. Watching from the doorway, where he has been guarding Jane from "murder hammers," Thori quietly asks, "why you…murder self?"

[17] *The Mighty Thor*, vol. 2, #705 (May 2018). All events and quotes are from this issue until further notice. (Quite an issue!)

[18] *The Mighty Thor*, vol. 2, #706 (June 2018); everything that follows, until it says otherwise, is drawn from this issue.

[19] Do you know who *is* worthy to wield a small piece of Mjolnir? Puddlegulp the frog, who befriended the Odinson in New York City's Central Park after Loki turned the Thunder God himself into a frog (*Thor*, vol. 1, #364, February 1986). Puddlegulp later lifted a tiny shard of Mjolnir, which transformed into the tiny hammer Frogjolnir and turned him into the Mighty Throg (*Lockjaw and the Pet Avengers* #1, July 2009). In *The Mighty Thor*, vol. 2, #700 (December 2017), Throg saves the life of Jane Foster, who was trapped under the wreckage of a building

while Mjolnir, on her command, searched for survivors. As she is about to transform back to her mortal form and be crushed, Throg arrives—causing her to mumble, "must be passing out…because I swear that frog…frog looks just like…"—and lets her touch his tiny hammer, transforming her back into Thor. If you think about it, without Throg, Jane may not have survived to defeat the Mangog and save the world. All hail the Mighty Throg!

[20] See also *Thor*, vol. 5, #7 (January 2019), a flashback to when Odin wanted young Thor to spend less time on Earth. Loki, always "helpful," causes his brother to fall in love with a mortal, Erika the Red, so he would learn heartbreak when she dies and abandon Earth forever. However, this experience only teaches Thor to value life all the more: "Cherish every moment. And every mortal soul you touch along the way. Cherish this all the more because they are fleeting. And you are not. That is the legacy of Erika the Red. The woman who taught Thor what it meant to be a god. What it meant to be worthy."

[21] *Generations: The Unworthy Thor & The Mighty Thor* #1. She adds, referencing her own struggle to preserve her humanity in the face of being needed as Thor, "Thank you for reminding me…why I should never let go." The Odinson's ties to Earth and humanity have been emphasized through his entire history, but for a particularly poignant treatment, see the 1988 graphic novel *Thor: I, Whom the Gods Would Destroy.*

[22] *Thor*, vol. 5, #1 (August 2018), "God of Thunder Reborn." When Thor visits Jane on Earth, she gushes over his new hammer, asking to touch it, "just a little," but Thor refuses until she is cancer-free. (It won't be long: We learn her cancer is in remission in *Thor*, vol. 5, #11, May 2019.)

[23] *Thor*, vol. 5, #3 (September 2018).

[24] Ibid.

[25] *Thor*, vol. 5, #8 (February 2019).

[26] *Thor*, vol. 5, #11.

[27] *War of the Realms* #5 (August 2019). Earlier in the battle, Jane received an even greater honor: Freyja named her the All-Mother of Asgard before leaving for Jotunheim, the Realm of the Giants, to rescue her son (*War of the Realms* #2, June 2019).

[28] *Thor*, vol. 5, #14 (August 2019).

[29] *War of the Realms* #5.

[30] *War of the Realms* #6 (August 2019).

[31] Ibid.

[32] Ibid.

[33] Ibid.

Epilogue

As things on Asgard settle into a new status quo following the War of the Realms, Thor addresses his returned Mjolnir in a revealing monologue.[1] It begins with a recognition that he can no longer take his worthiness for granted:

> I was lost without you. More than I ever had been before. 'Twas a hard lesson to learn. Especially for a god who moves moons and holds thunderstorms in his hands. Even after all these many years, after a life lived among the highest heavens and the nethermost hells...worthiness is a fragile thing. And so the Hel is the Mighty Thor.

He also knows now that worthiness is an ongoing process, and he must constantly strive to prove his worth and ensure that Gorr's statement that "no god is worthy" is proven wrong.

> I pray...that never changes. The day I stop struggling to be worthy is the day I lose the storm for good. And the day...Gorr is proven right once and for all.

He tells Mjolnir that it is more mysterious to him than ever, but he knows it is alive, and they are both beginning a new chapter in their lives together.

> I know not what you are anymore, Mjolnir. It was the storm of the four Thors that brought you back. That reforged you in the sun. And I can feel some remnant of the God Tempest still roaring inside you. As before, you are no mere enchanted chunk of Uru. You are alive. Just as sure as you've given life to me. We are bound in blood and thunder forever, my friend. Both of us reborn, renewed.

Finally, he acknowledges the existentialist imperative to recreate himself authentically when he says, "And now, with the great war finally at an end, together we must decide…who we are meant to be." No longer is he going to cede authority over his self-worth to the hammer, but he will form his new self *alongside* it, similar to how two people in a close relationship can continue to develop as autonomous individuals, separately and together at the same time.

While he does this, it will also be in a new role. Thor may no longer need the approval of his father, but after defeating Malekith and ending the War of the Realms, he gets it nonetheless: Odin tells him "well done" before kneeling before his son and proclaiming him the new All-Father of Asgard.[2] Not only that, but before the young Thor and King Thor return to their respective eras, Odin embraces all three versions of his son and tells them, "Odin is proud of you, Thor. In the name of all the gods…I am proud of my son."[3] Later, at the coronation celebration that Thor skips in favor of helping the people of the Ten Realms—including taking the buffet to the starving Dark Elves of Svartalfheim, much to the dismay of Volstagg—Odin tells Freyja that their son "showed us how to fall with grace. And rise again…stronger than ever. How to rise above our unworthiness. By owning it."[4] It seems even an old god such as Odin can learn new tricks, accepting Gorr's word and the paradoxical nature of worthiness through unworthiness. (Freyja, of course, knew these things long ago.)

And…what of Jane Foster? After hurling the Ultimate Universe Mjolnir through the head of Laufey, King of the Frost Giants—freeing his son Loki from his gullet and making him his successor—she reverts to her mortal form as she watches the hammer disintegrate and recast itself as a bracelet on her wrist.[5] Later, as she visits the deceased Valkyries in a New York City morgue, all of them having perished in the war, Thor appears to "bear my people to rest." Jane assumes he's taking them to

Valhalla, but Thor explains that, with no Valkyries to accompany fallen warriors there, Valhalla is no more. Jane senses his despair and wants to help him, thinking to herself, "if Asgard needs a Valkyrie," when the ghosts of the Valkyries appear and ask her, "Will you shoulder our burden?" Jane agrees, and the bracelet formed out of the Ultimate Universe Mjolnir is revealed to be Undrjarn the All-Weapon, which transforms her into the new Valkyrie, serving Asgard, Earth, and the rest of the Ten Realms in a new identity, but as the same hero she has always been—before, during, and after her time as the Mighty Thor.[6]

****

In his final scene in the last issue of Jason Aaron's epic run chronicling his adventures, the new All-Father Thor looks at Mjolnir, resting on his throne in Asgard, and says to it, "You know I leave you here each night for a reason, right? Because if I can't move you out of the way...then I don't deserve to sit there. So let's see where we are today then, shall we?" After he successfully lifts the hammer, he says, "All-Father it is. For another morn at least. So be it."[7] Even after ascending to the throne of Asgard, Thor never forgets that worthiness is not guaranteed, but must be earned every day through making the effort to maintain it.

Aaron expresses the same idea in his text piece at this end of this issue, in which he bids farewell to the character he has shepherded for seven years and expresses his gratitude to his artistic and editorial collaborators throughout his run. There, he describes the god he'd like to believe in, one "who lives every day questioning their own worthiness, aspiring for it, while also embracing their unworthiness, their failings."[8] This is not only the highest standard for a god, but for us mortals as well. We must not wallow in our inadequacies to such a degree that we never aspire to overcome them, nor should we grow so proud in our accom-plishments, or comfortable with our goodness, that we forget that these are but momentary achievements, much easier to lose than they were to attain. We must always try to do better and to be better—whatever that means for each one of us—and never rely on anyone else to tell us if we've done enough.

And if we have to wonder if we're doing enough…then we most likely are.

Verily!

---

[1] All of the following speech comes from *Thor*, vol. 5, #15 (September 2019).

[2] *War of the Realms* #6 (August 2019)

[3] *Thor*, vol. 5, #15.

[4] *Thor*, vol. 5, #16 (October 2019).

[5] *War of the Realms* #6.

[6] *War of the Realms Omega* #1 (September 2019); Jane's new adventures began the same month in *Valkyrie: Jane Foster* #1.

[7] *King Thor* #4 (February 2020).

[8] Ibid.

Reading Guide for the *Thor* Comics

As with most long-running superhero characters, understanding their publication history, especially in the last quarter-century, can be confusing. Unfortunately, Thor was not introduced in a *Thor* #1 comic, which then published sequentially month and month, year after year, until reaching the high triple digits in the present day. In fact, there was no issue number one of *Thor* until the second volume of his title, launched in 1998. Even *Fantastic Four* and *Avengers*, which both began with number-one issues, have been relaunched with new number-ones many times—but with Thor, we get the additional complication of changes in the book's title as well.

Thor's publication history began in **Journey into Mystery,** a horror, science fiction, and fantasy anthology title that began publication in 1952 during the Atlas Comics era. In August 1962, *Journey into Mystery* #83 featured a "new" character named Thor (although a version of the character more accurate to the Norse myths appeared in the Atlas title *Venus* in 1951). The adventures of Thor, as well as his eventual back-up feature "Tales of Asgard," which was introduced in issue #97 (October 1963), gradually came to dominate the book, until it was renamed *Thor* with issue #126 (March 1966).

This first volume of *Thor* lasted until issue #502 in September 1996, and continued for eleven more issues as *Journey into Mystery* #503-513, featuring other Asgardians, while Thor, several of his fellow Avengers, and the Fantastic Four became "Heroes Reborn" in another dimension. This was followed by "Heroes Return" in 1998 when they all…well, you know…at which point **the second volume of *Thor*** began with the character's first number-one issue in July. This volume lasted until issue #85 (December 2004), when a Ragnarok event destroyed Asgard, resulting in the death of most of the Asgardians (at least as much as Asgardians can be killed, given the revolving door to Valhalla).

The character of Thor then took some time off from regular publication, during which the heroes of the Marvel Universe had a Civil War that involved a clone of Thor that killed Bill Foster, the hero known as Goliath. Afterwards, **the third volume of *Thor*** began with a new number-one issue in September 2007, which lasted a mere twelve issues before its *legacy numbering*—the issue number that would have been reached had the original series not been renumbered several times in the interim—was restored, and the April 2009 comic that would have been issue #13 of volume 3 was now issue #600.

(Some bibliographers return to volume one when a comic book title reverts to its legacy numbering, but I prefer to retain the current volume so the volumes stay in order: Going from volume 3, issue #13, to volume 1, issue #600, in a list of issues just hurts my brain. In my opinion, issue numbers can roll back to #1, but volume number should always move forward.)

Volume 3 continued until issue #621 (May 2011), after which its numbering continued once again under the new (old) title of *Journey into Mystery*, featuring stories of first Loki and then Sif, from issue #622 (June 2011) to issue #655 (October 2013). Thor himself moved to **the first volume of *The Mighty Thor***, which started with issue #1 in June 2011 and ran through issue #22 in December 2012.

January 2013 saw the publication of the first issue of ***Thor: God of Thunder***, which was the beginning of writer Jason Aaron's seven-year run on the character (the main focus of this book). This run lasted until issue #25 (November 2014), after the *Original Sin* event in which Nick Fury whispered in the Odinson's ear and Jane picked up the hammer, becoming the Goddess of Thunder in the first issue of **the fourth volume of *Thor*** in December 2014.

This run lasted only eight issues—culminating in the revelation of the new Thor's identity—before it was interrupted by 2015's *Secret Wars* event (including a *Thors* miniseries), in which the Marvel Multiverse was destroyed and then put back together again. (Whew.) Jane's saga resumed in the **second volume of *The Mighty Thor***, which started with issue #1 in January 2016, while the Odinson's struggles with unworthiness were told in the five-issue miniseries ***The Unworthy Thor*** (January-May 2017). Before this volume of *The Mighty Thor* could reach issue #24 in December 2017, the legacy numbering kicked in once again, and it became issue #700 instead. This series only ran six more issues...for reasons...followed by a one-shot titled *The Mighty Thor: At the Gates of Valhalla* in July 2018...also for reasons...before the Odinson once again became the eponymous star of **the fifth volume of *Thor*** in its number one issue in August 2018.

This series ran until issue #16 in October 2019—most of it coincident with the *War of the Realms* miniseries and its many tie-in comics—and was followed by ***King Thor***, a four-issue miniseries recounting the final tale of the future Thor, which ran from November 2019 through February 2020 and represented Jason Aaron's final work on a *Thor* title (to date). He would, however, continue to write the character in *Avengers* for some time afterwards, while Donny Cates took over writing **the sixth volume of *Thor*** starting in March 2020, and Aaron, Al Ewing, and Torunn Grønbekk wrote Jane Foster's continuing adventures in a number of *Valkyrie* ongoing and limited series.

References

All comics cited in this book are listed below, along with their publication dates, writers, and artists (pencillers, inkers, and colorists); story titles are given only when there are multiple stories in the comic. Most of these comics have been collected in various hardcovers or trade paperbacks, available in hard copy or digital form, which I've listed as well. Most single issues are also available to buy digitally from Marvel.com or Comixology (and should be available through Marvel Unlimited as well).

All of the *Thor* comics written by Jason Aaron from 2013 to 2020—the focus of this book—have been collected several times, both in individual volumes as well as Complete Collections. Below, I list the individual volumes and note the Complete Collections like so:

CC1: *Thor by Jason Aaron: The Complete Collection Volume 1* (2019)

CC2: *Thor by Jason Aaron: The Complete Collection Volume 2* (2020)

CC3: *Thor by Jason Aaron: The Complete Collection Volume 3* (2021)

CC4: *Thor by Jason Aaron: The Complete Collection Volume 4* (2021)

CC5: *Thor by Jason Aaron: The Complete Collection Volume 5* (2022)

Avengers, vol. 8, #28 (February 2020). Jason Aaron (w), Ed McGuinness, Mark Morales, Jason Keith, and Erick Arciniega (a). Collected in *Avengers by Jason Aaron Volume 6: Starbrand Reborn* (2020).

Avengers, vol. 8, #43 (May 2021). Jason Aaron (w), Javier Garrón and David Curiel (a). Collected in *Avengers by Jason Aaron Volume 8: Enter the Phoenix* (2021).

Civil War #2 (August 2006). Mark Millar (w), Steve McNiven, Dexter Vines, and Morry Hollowell (a). Collected in *Civil War* (2007).

Fear Itself #7 (December 2011), "Thor's Day." Matt Fraction (w), Stuart Immonen, Wade van Grawbadger, Dexter Vines, Laura Martin, Justin Ponsor, and Matt Milla (a). Collected in *Fear Itself* (2012).

Generations: The Unworthy Thor & The Mighty Thor #1 (October 2017). Jason Aaron (w), Mahmud Asrar and Jordie Bellaire (a). Collected in *Generations* (2017) and CC4.

Journey into Mystery, vol. 1, #83 (August 1962), "Thor the Mighty and the Stone Men from Saturn!" Stan Lee and Larry Leiber (w), Jack Kirby, Joe Sinnott, and Stan Goldberg (a). Collected in *Thor Epic Collection: The God of Thunder* (2014).

Journey into Mystery, vol. 1, #84 (September 1962), "The Might Thor vs. the Executioner." Larry Leiber (w), Jack Kirby, Dick Ayers, and Stan Goldberg (a). Collected in *Thor Epic Collection: The God of Thunder* (2014).

Journey into Mystery, vol. 1, #94 (July 1963), "Thor and Loki Attack the Human Race!" Stan Lee and Robert Bernstein (w), Joe Sinnott (a). Collected in *Thor Epic Collection: The God of Thunder* (2014).

Journey into Mystery, vol. 1, #95 (August 1963), "The Demon Duplicators." Stan Lee and Robert Bernstein (w), Joe Sinnott and Stan Goldberg (a). Collected in *Thor Epic Collection: The God of Thunder* (2014).

Journey into Mystery, vol. 1, #99 (December 1963), "The Mysterious Mister Hyde!" Stan Lee (w) and Don Heck (a). Collected in *Thor Epic Collection: The God of Thunder* (2014).

Journey into Mystery, vol. 1, #100 (January 1964), "The Master Plan of Mr. Hyde!" Stan Lee (w) and Don Heck (a). Collected in *Thor Epic Collection: The God of Thunder* (2014).

Journey into Mystery, vol. 1, #100 (January 1964), "Tales of Asgard: The Storm Giants." Stan Lee (w), Jack Kirby and Paul Reinman (a). Collected in *Thor Epic Collection: The God of Thunder* (2014).

Journey into Mystery, vol. 1, #101 (February 1964). "Tales of Asgard: The Invasion of Asgard." Stan Lee (w), Jack Kirby and George Roussos (a). Collected in *Thor Epic Collection: The God of Thunder* (2014).

Journey into Mystery, vol. 1, #102 (March 1964). "Tales of Asgard: Death Comes to Thor." Stan Lee (w), Jack Kirby and Paul Reinman (a). Collected in *Thor Epic Collection: The God of Thunder* (2014).

Journey into Mystery, vol. 1, #112 (January 1965), "Tales of Asgard: The Coming of Loki!" Stan Lee (w), Jack Kirby and Vince Colletta (a). Collected in *Thor Epic Collection: When Titans Clash* (2016).

Journey into Mystery, vol. 1, #124 (January 1966), "The Grandeur and the Glory!" Stan Lee (w), Jack Kirby and Vince Colletta (a). Collected in *Thor Epic Collection: When Titans Clash* (2016).

Journey into Mystery, vol. 1, #632 (February 2012). Kieron Gillen (w), Mitch Breitweiser and Bettie Breitwesier (a). Collected in *Journey into Mystery by Kieron Gillen Complete Collection Volume 1* (2014).

King Thor #4 (February 2020). Jason Aaron (w), Gabriel Hernandez Walta, Andrea Sorrentino, Chris Burnham, Nick Pitarra, Aaron Kuder, Olivier Coipel, Russell Dauterman, Mike del Mundo, Chris O'Halloran, Dave Stewart, Nathan Fairbairn, Michael Garland, Laura Martin, and Matthew Wilson (a). Collected in *King Thor* (2020) and CC5.

Lockjaw and the Pet Avengers #1 (July 2009). Chris Eliopoulos (w), Ig Guara and Chris Sotomayor (a). Collected in *Lockjaw and the Pet Avengers* (2010).

The Mighty Thor, vol. 1, #1 (June 2011). Matt Fraction (w), Olivier Coipel, Mark Morales, Laura Martin, Justin Ponsor, and Peter Steigerwald (a). Collected in *The Mighty Thor, Volume 1* (2012).

The Mighty Thor, vol. 2, #1 (January 2016). Jason Aaron (w), Russell Dauterman and Matthew Wilson (a). Collected in *Mighty Thor Volume 1: Thunder in Her Veins* (2017) and CC3.

The Mighty Thor, vol. 2, #3 (March 2016). Jason Aaron (w), Russell Dauterman and Matthew Wilson (a). Collected in *Mighty Thor Volume 1: Thunder in Her Veins* (2017) and CC3.

The Mighty Thor, vol. 2, #4 (April 2016). Jason Aaron (w), Russell Dauterman and Matthew Wilson (a). Collected in *Mighty Thor Volume 1: Thunder in Her Veins* (2017) and CC3.

The Mighty Thor, vol. 2, #5 (May 2016). Jason Aaron (w), Russell Dauterman and Matthew Wilson (a). Collected in *Mighty Thor Volume 1: Thunder in Her Veins* (2017) and CC3.

The Mighty Thor, vol. 2, #8 (August 2016). Jason Aaron (w), Russell Dauterman and Matthew Wilson (a). Collected in *Mighty Thor Volume 2: Lords of Midgard* (2017) and CC3.

The Mighty Thor, vol. 2, #9 (September 2016). Jason Aaron (w), Russell Dauterman and Matthew Wilson (a). Collected in *Mighty Thor Volume 2: Lords of Midgard* (2017) and CC3.

The Mighty Thor, vol. 2, #10 (October 2016). Jason Aaron (w), Russell Dauterman and Matthew Wilson (a). Collected in *Mighty Thor Volume 2: Lords of Midgard* (2017) and CC3.

The Mighty Thor, vol. 2, #11 (November 2016). Jason Aaron (w), Russell Dauterman and Matthew Wilson (a). Collected in *Mighty Thor Volume 2: Lords of Midgard* (2017) and CC3.

The Mighty Thor, vol. 2, #12 (December 2016). Jason Aaron (w), Russell Dauterman, Frazer Irving, and Matthew Wilson (a). Collected in *Mighty Thor Volume 2: Lords of Midgard* (2017) and CC3.

The Mighty Thor, vol. 2, #16 (April 2017). Jason Aaron (w), Russell Dauterman and Matthew Wilson (a). Collected in *Mighty Thor Volume 3: The Asgard/Shi'ar War* (2018) and CC3.

The Mighty Thor, vol. 2, #19 (July 2017). Jason Aaron (w), Russell Dauterman, Valerio Schiti, Matthew Wilson, and Mat Lopes (a). Collected in *Mighty Thor Volume 3: The Asgard/Shi'ar War* (2018) and CC3.

The Mighty Thor, vol. 2, #20 (August 2017). Jason Aaron (w), Russell Dauterman, Valerio Schiti, Matthew Wilson, and Veronica Gandini (a). Collected in *Mighty Thor Volume 4: War Thor* (2018) and CC4.

The Mighty Thor, vol. 2, #21 (September 2017). Jason Aaron (w), Valerio Schiti and Veronica Gandini (a). Collected in *Mighty Thor Volume 4: War Thor* (2018) and CC4.

The Mighty Thor, vol. 2, #23 (November 2017). Jason Aaron (w), Valerio Schiti and Rain Beredo (a). Collected in *Mighty Thor Volume 4: War Thor* (2018) and CC4.

The Mighty Thor, vol. 2, #700 (December 2017). Jason Aaron (w), Walter Simonson, Russell Dauterman, Daniel Acuña, James Harren, Becky Cloonan, Das Pastorius, Chris Burnham, Andrew McLean, Jill Thompson, Mike del Mundo, Olivier Coipel, Matthew Wilson, Dave Stewart, and Ive Svorcina (a). Collected in *Mighty Thor Volume 5: The Death of the Mighty Thor* (2018) and CC4.

The Mighty Thor, vol. 2, #702 (February 2018). Jason Aaron (w), Russell Dauterman and Matthew Wilson (a). Collected in *Mighty Thor Volume 5: The Death of the Mighty Thor* (2018) and CC4.

The Mighty Thor, vol. 2, #703 (March 2018). Jason Aaron (w), Russell Dauterman and Matthew Wilson (a). Collected in *Mighty Thor Volume 5: The Death of the Mighty Thor* (2018) and CC4.

The Mighty Thor, vol. 2, #704 (April 2018). Jason Aaron (w), Russell Dauterman and Matthew Wilson (a). Collected in *Mighty Thor Volume 5: The Death of the Mighty Thor* (2018) and CC4.

The Mighty Thor, vol. 2, #705 (May 2018). Jason Aaron (w), Russell Dauterman and Matthew Wilson (a). Collected in *Mighty Thor Volume 5: The Death of the Mighty Thor* (2018) and CC4.

The Mighty Thor, vol. 2, #706 (June 2018). Jason Aaron (w), Russell Dauterman and Matthew Wilson (a). Collected in *Mighty Thor Volume 5: The Death of the Mighty Thor* (2018) and CC4.

The Mighty Thor: At the Gates of Valhalla #1 (July 2018). Jason Aaron (w), Jen Bartel, Ramón Pérez, and Matthew Wilson (a). Collected in *Mighty Thor Volume 5: The Death of the Mighty Thor* (2018) and CC4.

Original Sin #5.1 (September 2014). Jason Aaron and Al Ewing (w), Lee Garbett, Simone Bianchi, and Nolan Woodard (a). Collected in *Original Sin: Thor & Loki – The Tenth Realm* (2014).

Original Sin #5.2 (September 2014). Jason Aaron and Al Ewing (w), Lee Garbett, Simone Bianchi, and Adriano Dall'Alpi (a). Collected in *Original Sin: Thor & Loki – The Tenth Realm* (2014).

Original Sin #7 (October 2014). Jason Aaron (w), Mike Deodato, Jr., and Frank Martin, Jr. (a). Collected in *Original Sin* (2015).

Siege #3 (May 2010). Brian Michael Bendis (w), Olivier Coipel, Mark Morales, and Laura Martin (a). Collected in *Siege* (2010).

Thor, vol. 1, #136 (January 1967), "To Become an Immortal!" Stan Lee (w), Jack Kirby and Vince Colletta (a). Collected in *Thor Epic Collection: The Wrath of Odin* (2017).

Thor, vol. 1, #159 (December 1968). Stan Lee (w), Jack Kirby and Vince Colletta (a). Collected in *Thor Epic Collection: To Wake the Mangog* (2015).

Thor, vol. 1, #161 (February 1969). Stan Lee (w), Jack Kirby and Vince Colletta (a). Collected in *Thor Epic Collection: To Wake the Mangog* (2015).

Thor, vol. 1, #183 (December 1970). Stan Lee (w), John Buscema and Joe Sinnott (a). Collected in *Thor Epic Collection: The Fall of Asgard* (2018).

Thor, vol. 1, #231 (January 1975). Gerry Conway (w), John Buscema, Dick Giordano, and Petra Goldberg (a). Collected in *Thor Epic Collection: Ulik Unchained* (2021)

Thor, vol. 1, #236 (June 1975). Gerry Conway (w), John Buscema, Joe Sinnott, and Phil Rache (a). Collected in *Thor Epic Collection: Ulik Unchained* (2021)

Thor, vol. 1, #241 (November 1975). Bill Mantlo (w), John Buscema, Joe Sinnott, and Phil Rache (a). Collected in *Thor Epic Collection: Ulik Unchained* (2021)

Thor, vol. 1, #242 (December 1975). Len Wein (w), John Buscema, Joe Sinnott, and Glynis Wein (a). Collected in *Thor Epic Collection: War of the Gods* (2022)

Thor, vol. 1, #249 (July 1976). Len Wein (w), John Buscema, Tony DeZuniga, and Glynis Wein (a). Collected in *Thor: If Asgard Should Perish* (2010) and *Thor Epic Collection: War of the Gods* (2022)

Thor, vol. 1, #250 (August 1976). Len Wein (w), John Buscema, Tony DeZuniga, and Glynis Wein (a). Collected in *Thor: If Asgard Should Perish* (2010) and *Thor Epic Collection: War of the Gods* (2022).

Thor, vol. 1, #252 (October 1976), "Tales of Asgard: The Weapon and the Warrior." David Kraft (w), Pablo Marcos and Glynis Wein (a). Collected in *Thor: If Asgard Should Perish* (2010) and *Thor Epic Collection: War of the Gods* (2022).

Thor, vol. 1, #279 (January 1979). Don Glut (w), Alan Kupperberg, Pablo Marcos, and Glynis Wein (a).

Thor, vol. 1, #303 (January 1981). Doug Moench (w), Rick Leonardi, Chic Stone, and George Roussos (a). Collected in *Thor Epic Collection: A Kingdom Lost* (2014).

Thor, vol. 1, #330 (April 1983). Alan Zelenetz and Bob Hall (w), Bob Hall, Vince Colletta, and George Roussos (a). Collected in *Thor Epic Collection: Runequest* (2016).

Thor, vol. 1, #331 (May 1983). Alan Zelenetz and Bob Hall (w), Bob Hall, Vince Colletta, and George Roussos (a). Collected in *Thor Epic Collection: Runequest* (2016).

Thor, vol. 1, #334 (August 1983). Alan Zelenetz (w), Mark Bright, Vince Colletta, and George Roussos (a). Collected in *Thor Epic Collection: Runequest* (2016).

Thor, vol. 1, #335 (September 1983). Alan Zelenetz (w), Mark Bright, Vince Colletta, and George Roussos (a). Collected in *Thor Epic Collection: Runequest* (2016).

Thor, vol. 1, #336 (October 1983), "Of Gods and Men." Alan Zelenetz (w), Mark Bright, Vince Colletta, and George Roussos (a). Collected in *Thor Epic Collection: Runequest* (2016).

Thor, vol. 1, #337 (November 1983). Walter Simonson (w), Walter Simonson and George Roussos (a). Collected in *Thor by Walter Simonson Volume 1* (2017).

Thor, vol. 1, #338 (December 1983). Walter Simonson (w), Walter Simonson and George Roussos (a). Collected in *Thor by Walter Simonson Volume 1* (2017).

Thor, vol. 1, #339 (January 1984). Walter Simonson (w), Walter Simonson and George Roussos (a). Collected in *Thor by Walter Simonson Volume 1* (2017).

Thor, vol. 1, #340 (February 1984). Walter Simonson (w), Walter Simonson and George Roussos (a). Collected in *Thor by Walter Simonson Volume 1* (2017).

Thor, vol. 1, #364 (February 1986). Walter Simonson (w), Walter Simonson and Paul Becton (a). Collected in *Thor by Walter Simonson Volume 4* (2018).

Thor, vol. 1, #390 (April 1988). Tom DeFalco (w), Ron Frenz, Brett Breeding, and Christine Scheele (a). Collected in *Thor Epic Collection: War of the Pantheons* (2013).

Thor, vol. 1, #400 (February 1989), "I...This Hammer! (Or, If You Knew Uru Like We Know Uru!)" Tom DeFalco (w), Ron Frenz and Brett Breeding (a). Collected in *Thor Epic Collection: War of the Pantheons* (2013).

Thor, vol. 1, #415 (March 1990). Tom DeFalco (w), Herb Trimpe and George Roussos (a). Collected in *Thor Epic Collection: In Mortal Flesh* (2017).

Thor, vol. 1, #475 (June 1994). Roy Thomas (w), M.C. Wyman, Mike DeCarlo, and Ovi Hondru (a).

Thor, vol. 1, #481 (December 1994). Roy Thomas (w), M.C. Wyman, Mike DeCarlo, and Ovi Hondru (a).

Thor, vol. 1, #493 (December 1995). Warren Ellis (w), Mike Deodato, Jr., and Marie Javins (a). Collected in *Thor Epic Collection: Worldengine* (2018).

Thor, vol. 1, #502 (September 1996). William Messner-Loebs (w), Mike Deodato, Jr., Deodato Studios, and Marie Javins (a). Collected in *Thor Epic Collection: Worldengine* (2018).

Thor, vol. 2, #1 (July 1998). Dan Jurgens (w), John Romita, Jr., Klaus Janson, and Gregory Wright (a). Collected in *Thor by Dan Jurgens and John Romita Jr. Volume 1* (2009).

Thor, vol. 2, #21 (March 2000). Dan Jurgens (w), John Romita, Jr., Klaus Janson, and Gregory Wright (a). Collected in *Thor by Dan Jurgens and John Romita Jr. Volume 4* (2010).

Thor, vol. 2, #39 (September 2001). Dan Jurgens (w), Stuart Immonen, Wade von Grawbadger, and Dave Kemp (a). Collected in *Thor: The Death of Odin* (2011).

Thor, vol. 2, #51 (September 2002). Dan Jurgens (w), Tom Raney, Scott Hanna, and Dave Kemp (a). Collected in *Thor: Gods on Earth* (2011).

Thor, vol. 2, #64 (July 2003). Dan Jurgens (w), Paco Medina, Juan Vlasco, and Brian Reber. Collected in *Thor: Spiral* (2011).

Thor, vol. 2, #66 (September 2003). Dan Jurgens (w), Tom Mandrake and Brian Reber (a). Collected in *Thor: Spiral* (2011).

Thor, vol. 2, #79 (July 2004). Dan Jurgens (w), Scot Eaton, Drew Geraci, and Avalon Studios (a). Collected in *Thor: Gods & Men* (2011).

Thor, vol. 3, #1 (September 2007). J. Michael Straczynski (w), Olivier Coipel, Mark Morales, and Laura Martin (a). Collected in *Thor by J. Michael Straczynski Volume 1* (2008).

Thor, vol. 3, #8 (June 2008). J. Michael Straczynski (w), Marko Djurdjević, Danny Miki, Crimelab Studios, and Laura Martin (a). Collected in *Thor by J. Michael Straczynski Volume 2* (2009).

Thor, vol. 3, #10 (September 2008). J. Michael Straczynski (w), Olivier Coipel, Mark Morales, Allen Martinez, Victor Olazaba, and Laura Martin (a). Collected in *Thor by J. Michael Straczynski Volume 2* (2009).

Thor, vol. 3, #615 (November 2010). Matt Fraction (w), Pasqual Ferry and Matt Hollingsworth (a). Collected in *Thor: The World Eaters* (2011).

Thor, vol. 4, #1 (December 2014). Jason Aaron (w), Russell Dauterman and Matthew Wilson (a). Collected in *Thor Volume 1: The Goddess of Thunder* (2016) and CC2.

Thor, vol. 4, #2 (January 2015). Jason Aaron (w), Russell Dauterman and Matthew Wilson (a). Collected in *Thor Volume 1: The Goddess of Thunder* (2016) and CC2.

Thor, vol. 4, #3 (February 2015). Jason Aaron (w), Russell Dauterman and Matthew Wilson (a). Collected in *Thor Volume 1: The Goddess of Thunder* (2016) and CC2.

Thor, vol. 4, #4 (March 2015). Jason Aaron (w), Russell Dauterman and Matthew Wilson (a). Collected in *Thor Volume 1: The Goddess of Thunder* (2016) and CC2.

Thor, vol. 4, #5 (April 2015). Jason Aaron (w) and Jorge Molina (a). Collected in *Thor Volume 1: The Goddess of Thunder* (2016) and CC2.

Thor, vol. 4, #6 (May 2015). Jason Aaron (w), Russell Dauterman and Matthew Wilson (a). Collected in *Thor Volume 2: Who Holds the Hammer?* (2016) and CC2.

Thor, vol. 4, #8 (July 2015). Jason Aaron (w), Russell Dauterman and Matthew Wilson (a). Collected in *Thor Volume 2: Who Holds the Hammer?* (2016) and CC2.

Thor, vol. 5, #1 (August 2018), "God of Thunder Reborn." Jason Aaron (w), Mike del Mundo and Marco D'Alfonson (a). Collected in *Thor Volume 1: God of Thunder Reborn* (2018) and CC5.

Thor, vol. 5, #3 (September 2018). Jason Aaron (w), Mike del Mundo and Marco D'Alfonso (a). Collected in *Thor Volume 1: God of Thunder Reborn* (2018) and CC5.

Thor, vol. 5, #7 (January 2019). Jason Aaron (w), Tony Moore and John Rauch (a). Collected in *Thor Volume 2: Road to War of the Realms* (2019) and CC5.

Thor, vol. 5, #8 (February 2019). Jason Aaron (w) and Mike del Mundo (a). Collected in *Thor Volume 2: Road to War of the Realms* (2019) and CC5.

Thor, vol. 5, #9 (March 2019). Jason Aaron (w) and Mike del Mundo (a). Collected in *Thor Volume 2: Road to War of the Realms* (2019) and CC5.

Thor, vol. 5, #11 (May 2019). Jason Aaron (w), Lee Garbett and Antonio Fabela (a). Collected in *Thor Volume 2: Road to War of the Realms* (2019) and CC5.

Thor, vol. 5, #14 (August 2019). Jason Aaron (w), Scott Hepburn and Matthew Wilson (a). Collected in *Thor Volume 3: War's End* (2019) and CC5.

Thor, vol. 5, #15 (September 2019). Jason Aaron (w), Mike del Mundo and Marco D'Alfonso (a). Collected in *Thor Volume 3: War's End* (2019) and CC5.

Thor, vol. 5, #16 (October 2019). Jason Aaron (w), Mike del Mundo and Marco D'Alfonso (a). Collected in *Thor Volume 3: War's End* (2019) and CC5.

Thor Annual, vol. 1, #9 (1981). Chris Claremont (w), Luke McDonnell, Vince Colletta, and Bonnie Wilford (a). Collected in *Thor Epic Collection: A Kingdom Lost* (2014).

Thor Annual, vol. 1, #11 (1983). Alan Zelenetz (w), Bob Hall, Vince Colletta, and Carl Gafford (a). Collected in *Thor Epic Collection: Runequest* (2016).

Thor Annual, vol. 1, #14 (1989), "Relative Strengths and Comparisons." Peter Sanderson (w), Ron Lim and Mike DeCarlo (a). Collected in *Thor Epic Collection: In Mortal Flesh* (2017).

Thor Annual 2000, vol. 2 (2000), "Final Confrontation." Dan Jurgens (w), Jerry Ordway and Moose Baumann (a). Collected in *Thor by Dan Jurgens and John Romita Jr. Volume 4* (2010).

Thor Annual, vol. 4, #1 (April 2015), untitled second story. Noelle Stevenson (w) and Marguerite Savage (a). Collected in *Thor Volume 2: Who Holds the Hammer?* (2016) and CC2.

Thor: Blood Oath #1 (November 2005). Mike Avon Oeming (w), Scott Kolins and Wil Quintana (a). Collect in *Thor: Blood Oath* (2005).

Thor: Blood Oath #6 (February 2006). Mike Avon Oeming (w), Scott Kolins and Wil Quintana (a). Collect in *Thor: Blood Oath* (2005).

Thor: First Thunder #5 (March 2011). Bryan J. L. Glass (w), Tan Eng Huat, Victor Olazaba, and José Villarrubia (a). Collected in *Thor: First Thunder* (2011).

Thor: God of Thunder #1 (January 2013). Jason Aaron (w), Esad Ribić and Ive Svorcina (a). Collected in *Thor: God of Thunder Volume 1: The God Butcher* (2014) and CC1.

Thor: God of Thunder #2 (January 2013). Jason Aaron (w), Esad Ribić and Ive Svorcina (a). Collected in *Thor: God of Thunder Volume 1: The God Butcher* (2014) and CC1.

Thor: God of Thunder #3 (February 2013). Jason Aaron (w), Esad Ribić and Ive Svorcina (a). Collected in *Thor: God of Thunder Volume 1: The God Butcher* (2014) and CC1.

Thor: God of Thunder #4 (March 2013). Jason Aaron (w), Esad Ribić and Ive Svorcina (a). Collected in *Thor: God of Thunder Volume 1: The God Butcher* (2014) and CC1.

Thor: God of Thunder #6 (May 2013). Jason Aaron (w), Butch Guice, Tom Palmer, and Ive Svorcina (a). Collected in *Thor: God of Thunder Volume 2: Godbomb* (2014) and CC1.

Thor: God of Thunder #9 (August 2013). Jason Aaron (w), Esad Ribić and Ive Svorcina (a). Collected in *Thor: God of Thunder Volume 2: Godbomb* (2014) and CC1.

Thor: God of Thunder #10 (September 2013). Jason Aaron (w), Esad Ribić and Ive Svorcina (a). Collected in *Thor: God of Thunder Volume 2: Godbomb* (2014) and CC1.

Thor: God of Thunder #11 (October 2013). Jason Aaron (w), Esad Ribić and Ive Svorcina (a). Collected in *Thor: God of Thunder Volume 2: Godbomb* (2014) and CC1.

Thor: God of Thunder #12 (October 2013). Jason Aaron (w) and Nic Klein (a). Collected in *Thor: God of Thunder Volume 3: The Accursed* (2014) and CC1.

Thor: God of Thunder #17 (March 2014). Jason Aaron (w), Emanuela Lupacchino, Ron Garney, Ive Svorcina, and Lee Loughridge (a). Collected in *Thor: God of Thunder Volume 3: The Accursed* (2014) and CC1.

Thor: God of Thunder #24 (September 2014). Jason Aaron (w), Agustin Alessio, Esad Ribić, and Ive Svorcina (a). Collected in *Thor: God of Thunder Volume 4: The Last Days of Midgard* (2015) and CC2.

Thor: God of Thunder #25 (November 2014). Jason Aaron (w), Esad Ribić, R. M. Guéra, Simon Bisley, Ive Svorcina, and Giulia Brusco (a).

Collected in *Thor: God of Thunder Volume 4: The Last Days of Midgard* (2015) and CC2.

Thor: Godstorm #1 (November 2001). Kurt Busiek (w), Steve Rude, Mike Royer, and Greg Wright (a). Collected in *Thor: Godstorm* (2010).

Thor: Heaven & Earth #3 (October 2011). Paul Jenkins (w), Pascal Alixe and Sotocolor (a). Collected in *Thor: Heaven & Earth* (2011).

Thor: I, Whom the Gods Would Destroy (Marvel Graphic Novel #33, 1988). Jim Shooter and Jim Owsley (w), Paul Ryan, Vince Colletta, and Bob Sharen (a).

The Unworthy Thor #1 (January 2017). Jason Aaron (w), Olivier Coipel and Matthew Wilson (a). Collected in *The Unworthy Thor* (2017) and CC4.

The Unworthy Thor #2 (February 2017). Jason Aaron (w), Olivier Coipel and Matthew Wilson (a). Collected in *The Unworthy Thor* (2017) and CC4.

The Unworthy Thor #3 (March 2017). Jason Aaron (w), Olivier Coipel, Kim Jacinto, and Matthew Wilson (a). Collected in *The Unworthy Thor* (2017) and CC4.

The Unworthy Thor #4 (April 2017). Jason Aaron (w), Olivier Coipel, Frazer Irving, Esad Ribić, Russell Dauterman, Kim Jacinto, Matthew Wilson, and Matt Milla (a). Collected in *The Unworthy Thor* (2017) and CC4.

The Unworthy Thor #5 (May 2017). Jason Aaron (w), Olivier Coipel, Kim Jacinto, Pascal Alixe, Mat Lopes, and Jay David Ramos (a). Collected in *The Unworthy Thor* (2017) and CC4.

Valkyrie: Jane Foster #1 (September 2019). Jason Aaron and Al Ewing (w), Cafu and Jesus Aburtov (a). Collected in *Valkyrie: Jane Foster Volume 1: The Sacred and the Profane* (2020).

Venom, vol. 4, #4 (September 2018). Donny Cates (w), Ryan Stegman, JP Mayer, and Frank Martin, Jr. (a). Collected in *Venom by Donny Cates Volume 1: Rex* (2018).

War of the Realms #2 (June 2019). Jason Aaron (w), Russell Dauterman and Matthew Wilson (a). Collected in *War of the Realms* (2019).

War of the Realms #5 (August 2019). Jason Aaron (w), Russell Dauterman and Matthew Wilson (a). Collected in *War of the Realms* (2019).

War of the Realms #6 (August 2019). Jason Aaron (w), Russell Dauterman and Matthew Wilson (a). Collected in *War of the Realms* (2019).

War of the Realms Omega #1 (September 2019). Jason Aaron, Al Ewing, Daniel Kibblesmith, and Gerry Duggan (w), Ron Garney, Cafu, Oscar Bazaldua, Juan Ferreyra, Matt Milla, Jesus Aburtov, and David Curiel (a). The Jane Foster material referenced above is collected in *Valkyrie: Jane Foster Volume 1: The Sacred and the Profane* (2020).

What If?, vol. 1, #10 (August 1978). Don Glut (w), Rick Hoberg, Dave Hunt, and Carl Gafford (a). Collected in *Thor Volume 2: Who Holds the Hammer?* (2016) and *What If? Classic: The Complete Collection Volume 1* (2019).

About the Author

Mark D. White is the chair of the Department of Philosophy at the College of Staten Island/CUNY, where he teaches courses in philosophy, economics, and law. In addition to this one, he is the author of seven books—*A Philosopher Reads Marvel Comics' Civil War: Exploring the Moral Judgment of Captain America, Iron Man, and Spider-Man* (Ockham Publishing), *The Virtues of Captain America: Modern-Day Lessons on Character from a World War II Superhero* and *Batman and Ethics* (both from Wiley-Blackwell), *The Manipulation of Choice: Ethics and Libertarian Paternalism*, *The Illusion of Well-Being: Economic Policy-making Based on Respect and Responsiveness*, and *The Decline on the Individual: Reconciling Autonomy with Community* (all from Palgrave Macmillan), and *Kantian Ethics and Economics: Autonomy, Dignity, and Character* (Stanford University Press)—as well as over 60 academic journal articles and book chapters in the intersections between economics, philosophy, and law. He has also edited or co-edited a number of books on these subjects, including *The Oxford Handbook of Ethics and Economics*, *The Thief of Time: Philosophical Essays on Procrastination* (with Chrisoula Andreou), *Economics and the Virtues: Building a New Moral Foundation* (with Jennifer A. Baker), and *Retributivism: Essays on Theory and Policy* (all from Oxford University Press).

Mark is also a frequent contributor and editor in the Blackwell Philosophy and Pop Culture series, which introduces readers to basic philosophical concepts using the movies, TV shows, comic books, and music that they love. He has edited or co-edited volumes on Batman, *Watchmen*, Iron Man, Green Lantern, Superman, Doctor Strange, and the

Avengers, and contributed to volumes on Black Panther, Wonder Woman, Spider-Man, the X-Men, Black Sabbath, Metallica, *South Park*, *The Office*, *Family Guy*, and *Alice in Wonderland*.

You can find more information about Mark's books, articles, and blogs at http://www.profmdwhite.com and follow him on Twitter (@profmdwhite).